THE

BOOK

OF THE

STATES

☆

VINCENT WILSON, JR

Maps by
Peter L. Guilday

American History Research Associates
Brookeville, Maryland

Fourth Edition

Printed in the United States of America

BY

R. R. Donnelley & Sons Company

LIBRARY OF CONGRESS CATALOG CARD NO. 77-187584

American History Research Associates

BOX 140, BROOKEVILLE, MARYLAND

CONTENTS

INTRODUCTION

.

Over two centuries ago, thirteen English colonies took the unprecedented step of rebelling aginst the mother country and declaring their own independence. Only after lengthy debate and deliberation—and with some reluctance—did these independent "colonies" join in a loose confederation and, after 1787, become an infant nation. In two centuries, that nation has grown from thirteen to fifty States and become a mighty world power. In spite of its growth and recognition *as a nation,* the country is still very much a union of individual States, each with its own history—its unique story of settlement and growth.

In most regions, the States were confronted with similar problems: the first colonies faced not only the basic problem of establishing themselves in a new and unknown land, but also the unprecedented task of shaping a kind of government that suited the freedom of their new condition; in doing so, they created representative forms of government that were later to influence the design of the national government. These first States, as well as those that joined the already independent Federal Union and had a democratic form of government already developed for them, were also confronted with other kinds of problems—slavery, the Indians, and, in some cases, the challenges of Spaniards, Frenchmen, Mexicans and British.

Each State was built at great human cost, built of sacrifice and courage and, sometimes—to our shame—of duplicity and deceit. The Pilgrim Fathers, it has been said, fell first on their knees and then on the aborigines; and the white man's (and the nation's) treatment of the Indians from State to State, from treaty to treaty, must be recognized as a shameful chapter in U.S. history.

A part of the history of each State is preserved in its name —often a most distinctive characteristic. The names of the first colonies naturally reflect the influence of England (Jersey, York, Hampshire) and of English royalty (Carolina, Georgia, Maryland and Virginia), but the Indians left their mark on two of the original colonies (Massachusetts and Connecticut) and on most of the remaining States. The early influence of France and Spain has been preserved in Louisiana and Vermont, and in Florida, California and Nevada. Although there is a distressing sameness in the names of American cities (Note the number of Washingtons, Lincolns and Jeffersons), the States present a rich and colorful array of names, thanks largely to the number of different Indian tribes represented. Here, at least, the Indians—and traces of their culture—have remained dominant.

Had it not been for the political genius of Thomas Jefferson, who was primarily responsible for the Northwest Ordinance, and the men who in 1787 hammered out the Federal Constitution, the thirteen original colonies might have turned into thirteen small nations forever quarreling over boundaries, tariffs, rates of exchange of currencies,

6

etc. But that did not happen, first, because the Constitution brought the colonies together into the Federal Union, and, second, because the Northwest Ordinance permitted new States to be formed from the western territories *and to join the Union on an equal basis with the original States*—a dramatic departure from the Old World practice of colonization. It was, therefore, primarily the Northwest Ordinance that made possible the growth of a small coastal nation to one of continental proportions; it was that ordinance that offered a unique opportunity to oppressed peoples of the world: join our experiment in freedom, this legislation seemed to say; we have undeveloped territories and a federal system, one that is open to you if you wish to settle and eventually form a State. And people came from almost every country in the world to settle and, in time, to form new States.

The picture of the generous system that offered oppressed peoples a new kind of freedom and democracy is, unfortunately, flawed by the inescapable fact that the lands for this noble experiment were, in most areas, wrested from the Indians.

Whether the United States will go beyond the present fifty States, no one can say. For almost half a century the United States comprised the forty-eight contiguous States, but, with the admittance of Hawaii, the Federal system jumped the continental borders. It is always possible that some other U.S. Territory, such as Puerto Rico, or the Federal District of Columbia, will someday become a State, but the admittance of Hawaii and Alaska signaled more than the growth of the country: it demonstrated that the most equitable political system of expansion ever devised—one that permitted the United States to become the most powerful free nation in the world—is still very much alive.

ALABAMA

(Name of Indian tribe)

Creek, Choctaw, Chickasaw, Pineda, DeSoto, Le Moyne, Ft. Mims, Horseshoe Bend, Montgomery, Mobile Bay, Tuskegee, TVA, Carver, Redstone Arsenal

The Space Flight Center at Huntsville and the South's largest steel center at Birmingham show how far the "Cotton State" has come in the Twentieth century. Alabama was given that name over 100 years ago, when cotton was its major source of income; destruction by the boll weevil, and G. W. Carver's experiments with crop rotation led farmers to turn to other crops (corn, peanuts, soybeans), and during these years, the iron and steel industry grew around Birmingham, which has become the "Pittsburgh of the South."

Alabama's natural wealth provided a valuable base for its industrial growth: the northern section is one of the few areas of the world that has the three principal materials needed to make steel—coal, limestone, and iron ore. Dams on Alabama's rivers—some operated by the Tennessee Valley Authority—provide power for metal-processing plants and textile mills. And the State's forests support lumber and paper industries.

Alabama is made up of land that once belonged to France, Britain and Spain—and the Creek Nation. One of the Civilized Tribes, the Creeks were forcibly moved from their tribal lands to the West in the 1830's, in violation of formal treaties with the Federal Government. It is ironic that appeals by Creek chieftains to President Jackson were of no avail, for he had first gained national prominence years before when, aided by these friendly Creeks, he had defeated warring anti-American Creeks at Horseshoe Bend.

"The Heart of Dixie" played a key role in the Civil War. The Confederacy was established, and Jefferson Davis was inaugurated president, at Montgomery, the Confederate capital from February to May 1861. The only major conflict in the State was the battle of Mobile Bay in 1864, which closed the last Confederate port open to shipping.

Alabama today offers a heritage from the past—prehistoric mounds, over 2,000 ante-bellum mansions, and battle-scarred Ft. Morgan on Mobile Bay; a moderate climate; and such annual attractions as Mobile's Mardi Gras and its dazzling 35-mile Azalea Trail.

THE HEART OF DIXIE

POPULATION	DATE	HISTORIC EVENTS
	1519	Alonso de Pineda of Spain explored Mobile Bay
	1540	DeSoto explored interior, defeated Choctaws
	1702	Pierre and Jean LeMoyne built first permanent settlement, Ft. Louis
1,250	1800	
	1813	Bands of Creeks massacred settlers at Ft. Mims
	1814	Gen. Jackson defeated warring Creeks at Horseshoe Bend
	1817	Became Alabama Territory
	1819	Joined Union as 22nd State
127,901	1820	
	1836-7	Federal troops drove Indians from their lands
590,756	1840	
	1848	Alabama Platform denied Federal Government right to bar slaves from territories
	1861	Seceded from Union, Confederate States of America formed at Montgomery
	1864	Union Adm. Farragut won battle of Mobile Bay
	1868	Rejoined Union
1,262,505	1880	First blast furnace operated at Birmingham
	1881	Tuskegee Institute founded; directed by Booker T. Washington
	1915	Severe attack of boll weevil on cotton
2,348,174	1920	
	1941	Redstone Arsenal established at Huntsville
	1955	Martin Luther King led civil rights protest in Montgomery
3,266,740	1960	Space Flight Center established at Huntsville
	1963	National Guard enforced school desegregation
3,444,165	1970	

AREA: 51,609 sq. mi.

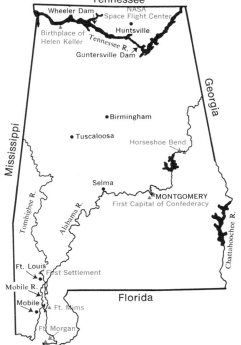

ALASKA

(Aleut: "greatland")

Eskimo, Bering, Cook, Seward,
Athabascan, Tlingit, Klondike,
Mt. McKinley, North Slope

The largest, coldest, most northerly State, Alaska is the only U.S. territory that once belonged to Russia, and it is by far the closest to Russia: only 55 miles separates the U.S. and the U.S.S.R. at the Bering Strait.

One-fifth the size of the nation it joined in 1959, Alaska brought to the Union a new frontier with unexplored tracts of wilderness, glaciers, volcanoes, and extensive mountain ranges—including the highest peak in North America, Mt. McKinley (20,320 Ft.). It is the only State with Eskimos, tundra, walrus, ptarmigan, and polar bears.

About one-quarter of Alaska's people are natives—Eskimo in the north; Athabascan in the interior; and Tlingit, Haida, and Tsimshian in the south. The Tlingits are famous for their carved totem poles.

Alaska grew up with the airplane, and flying is the chief means of transportation. Alaska has more private planes and pilots, per capita, than any other State, and jet service links it with Seattle and Chicago, as well as the Orient.

Alaska has vast natural resources: the Russians found valuable furs, and men of many nations made fortunes from silver, gold, platinum, copper and timber. Alaska has the largest coal reserves of any State. The famous Gold Rush of 1897 was surpassed by the Oil Rush of 1957, and today Alaska's fish—salmon, King crab, shrimp, and halibut—are one of its richest resources. Its big game—bear, moose and caribou—and its untouched natural beauty attract many visitors. Alaska has over three million lakes. Half of Alaska's population is concentrated in the Seward-Anchorage-Fairbanks region, which is served by the railroad. The potential resources of remote regions are still being assessed. Alaska is the nation's newest—and last—frontier.

POPULATION	DATE	HISTORIC EVENTS
	1741	Discovered by Vitus Bering, a Dane, leading expedition for Czar Peter the Great
	1775	Spanish landed at Sitka
	1778	Capt. Cook explored Alaska coast
	1786	French scientists explored area
	1788	First U.S. traders visited Alaska
	1799	Russian-American Co. established base at New Archangel
	1820	First U.S. whaling ships in Alaskan waters
	1867	Secretary of State Seward negotiated purchase for U.S. for $7,200,000
33,426	1880	Gold discovered at Juneau
	1884	Organic Act provided for governor, court, commissioners
	1896	Gold discovered in Klondike
64,356	1910	
	1912	Became Alaska Territory
	1923	Warren Harding, first U.S. President to visit Alaska
59,278	1930	
	1941	Work begun on Alcan Highway
128,643	1950	
	1957	Oil discovered on Kenai Peninsula
	1959	Alaska joined Union as 49th State
226,167	1960	
	1964	March 27—Severe earthquake at Anchorage
302,173	1970	

AREA: 596,400 sq. mi.

ARIZONA

48th

(Papago: "little spring")

Apache, Navajo, Hopi, Moqui,
Papago, de Niza, Coronado,
Tumacacori, Grand Canyon, Hoover Dam

Cut into the high plateau of northern Arizona, a mile deep and over 200 miles long, is the awesome Grand Canyon of the Colorado River. The Petrified Forest and the Painted Desert are other geologic marvels that were part of this land when prehistoric peoples lived in the almost inaccessible cliff dwellings that still exist. Later came Spanish conquistadores. But it was not until Americans came that the Arizona desert was transformed into a prosperous, growing land.

Discovery of rich copper deposits brought the first settlers to Arizona in the nineteenth century; the successful use of irrigation and the attractive climate brought many more in the twentieth. Dams built on the Colorado, Salt and Gila rivers provided water for the fertile valleys in the south; and farms, cattle ranches and towns sprang up. Today irrigated farms grow melons, citrus, vegetables and cotton. Mining remains important to Arizona: the State produces lead, zinc, silver, gold and uranium—and leads the nation in the production of copper.

American pioneers came to a land dominated by Indians—especially the Apaches, who, until 1886, threatened the peace of the Territory. Arizona now has the largest Indian population of any State, with thirteen tribes, including the Pima, Papago, Apache, Hopi, and Navajo—the largest tribe in the nation. Within its boundaries are more than half of all Indian lands in the U.S.

The State's principal cities—Phoenix, the capital, and Tucson—have grown rapidly since World War II. For decades they have attracted tourists and those seeking a dry climate; in addition, these cities have become industrial centers with major electronics and airplane plants.

With more sunshine than any other State, Arizona has a climate that rivals its natural wonders—one of the reasons it has become one of the fastest growing States in the Union.

POPULATION	DATE	HISTORIC EVENTS
	1593	Father Marcos de Niza first white man to explore area
	1540	Coronado explored Moqui country and Grand Canyon
	1680	Moqui revolted from Spanish
	1687	Father Kino established Tumacacori mission
	1776	Spanish established Tucson
	1800	Kit Carson, other Americans, explore area
	1821	Became part of newly independent Mexico
	1848	Area north of Gila River became part of U.S.
	1853	Gadsden Purchase—present southern border area acquired
	1854	Copper discovered
	1863	Became Arizona Territory; Prescott the capital
9,658	1870	
	1886	Final battles with Apaches
	1899	Phoenix made capital
122,931	1900	
	1911	Roosevelt Dam built
	1912	Became 48th State
	1915	Labor strikes in mines at Morence and Bisbee
334,162	1920	
	1936	Hoover Dam completed
1,302,161	1960	
1,772,482	1970	

AREA: 113,909 sq. mi.

ARKANSAS

(Sioux: "south-wind people")

25th

Arkansoa, De Soto, LaSalle,
DeTonti, Ozarks, Novaculite,
Bauxite, Murfreesboro, Little Rock

Arkansas has unique riches in—and below—its soil. In addition to extensive forests, Arkansas grows almost every crop produced in the U.S., and its mineral deposits—besides oil, gas and coal—include the nation's prime source of aluminum ore and the only diamond mine in North America.

Arkansas is almost evenly divided between the lowlands along the Mississippi and the rugged mountains in the west. Early in the nineteenth century, cotton planters moved into the rich lowlands, and cotton remains one of the principal crops, along with rice, corn and soybeans. For years, lumbering has been a leading industry: approximately one quarter of the State is covered with timber. Equally important are the cattle, hogs, and chickens raised in the high plateau in the northwest.

Although agriculture has long dominated Arkansas's economy, the Sixties saw manufacturing take first place. Today plants in the State make products from paper cups to cement, from shirts to rubber tires.

Arkansas's mineral resources were first exploited by the Indians. Years before the white man came, Indians were working the novaculite deposits near Malvern and Hot Springs, getting this hard, fine-grained stone for arrow heads, spear points, and knives. The State is still a prime source of novaculite, used now principally for whetstones. And from the town of Bauxite, which gave its name to aluminum ore, comes 95 per cent of that ore produced in the U.S. Most of Arkansas's oil fields are along its southern border, and the continent's only diamond mine is near Murfreesboro.

Arkansas has an abundance of lakes, streams and forests—including Ouachita and Ozark national forests. Famous health resorts are located at the State's exceptional natural springs; the most celebrated: Hot Springs.

14

POPULATION	DATE	HISTORIC EVENTS
	1541	DeSoto explored area
	1673	Marquette and Joliet visited Arkansas Indians
	1682	La Salle claimed area for France
	1686	DeTonti built first permanent settlement, Arkansas Post
	1763	France ceded area to Spain
	1801	Area returned to France
	1803	U.S. acquired area in Louisiana Purchase
1,062	1810	
	1819	Became Arkansas Territory
	1836	Joined Union as 25th State
97,574	1840	
	1861	Seceded from the Union
	1868	Rejoined the Union
484,471	1870	
	1874	Constitution adopted
	1887	Aluminum ore (Bauxite) discovered
1,128,211	1890	
	1906	Diamonds discovered near Murfreesboro
	1921	Oil discovered at El Dorado
1,854,482	1930	
	1957	Federal troops enforced school desegregation at Little Rock
1,923,295	1970	

AREA: 53,102 sq. mi.

15

CALIFORNIA

(Name of island in *Las Sergas de Esplandian*)

Cabrillo, Junipero Serra, Sutter's Mill,
Sierra Nevada, San Francisco, Hollywood,
Mt. Palomar, Oakland Bay Bridge

The fastest growing State, California has been the goal for many Americans since the Gold Rush, which in 1849 brought approximately 80,000 to the Territory. Ever since, the people have been coming: after 1870 the transcontinental railroads made it easier; in the 1920s the migration by automobile began. In the 1930s, families came from the Oklahoma Dust Bowl— so graphically depicted in *Grapes of Wrath;* and, since then, the rate of migration has soared as more and more people have come to work in industry, to farm, and to retire.

California combines a richness of resources, terrain and climate with vast agricultural enterprises, a variety of industries, a 1200-mile coastline, and several fine ports to form the Empire State of the West. Its exceptional natural assets include the snow-topped Sierra Nevada, fertile valleys, giant sequoia redwoods, the Mojave and Colorado deserts, San Francisco Bay and, beneath its surface, gold, silver, iron, and oil. National forests cover one fifth of the State. California seems to have everything— except water, but, through irrigation, it has become the leading U.S. grower of fruits and vegetables and the nation's prime producer of wines.

The early history of California is reflected in the twenty surviving Spanish missions and in place names like San Francisco and San Diego. When the thinly settled territory struggled to be free from Spain and Mexico, it weathered a few uncertain days as an independent republic and, with the end of the Mexican War, joined the U.S. Since then, California's growth has been continuous and rapid. From 1940 to 1960, its population more than doubled.

Now the most populous State, California continues to be the land of plenty: in the south—Hollywood, Mt. Palomar (largest reflector telescope), citrus groves, and a growing electronics and aviation center; in the north— extensive orchards, beef and dairy ranches, and one of the world's great ports. And, throughout the State, scenic splendor of every description— some of the reasons that Americans have continued to stream over the mountains to find the Golden State.

THE GOLDEN STATE

POPULATION	DATE	HISTORIC EVENTS
	1535	Cortez named area "California"
	1542	Juan Cabrillo credited with "discovery" of California
	1769	Fr. Junipero Serra began building 21 missions
	1806	Russians failed in attempt to found settlement in N. Calif.
	1810	Mexican revolution began; California loyal to Spain
	1822	Became part of Mexico
	1835	President Jackson offered to buy N. Calif.
	1845	Capt. J.C. Fremont provoked "Bear Flag War"
	1848	Mexico ceded California to U.S.
		Gold discovered at Sutter's Mill
92,597	1850	Joined Union as 31st State (a "free" State—part of Compromise of 1850)
1,213,398	1890	
	1906	Apr 18—Earthquake and fire destroyed large part of San Francisco
3,426,861	1920	Hollywood became film center of world
	1936	Bay Bridge opened—longest in world over navigable water
	1937	Golden Gate Bridge opened
6,907,387	1940	
	1945	United Nations' Charter drafted in San Francisco
10,586,223	1950	Earl Warren elected to unprecedented 3rd term as governor
15,717,204	1960	
19,953,134	1970	

AREA: 158,693 sq. mi.

COLORADO

(Spanish: "red")

*Pueblo, Ute, Arapahoe, Cheyenne, Pike,
San Luis, Rocky Flats, Grand Junction,
Air Force Academy, NORAD*

Highest State in the Union, Colorado encompasses part of the Continental Divide—the range of peaks that separates the rivers that flow east and west. Within its borders are 54 of the nation's highest mountains, including Pike's Peak (14,110 Ft.) and Mt. Elbert (14,431 Ft.), the second highest mountain in the contiguous States. At Mt. Evans is the Inter-University High-Altitude Laboratory; near Boulder is the National Center for Atmospheric Research.

For centuries bands of Cheyennes, Arapahoes, and Utes roamed the high plains of eastern Colorado, hunting buffalo and living in tipis, until the wagon trains came. Many of the Indians resisted the newcomers, the Cheyennes fighting a memorable battle against U.S. soldiers at Sand Creek (1864), the Utes conducting attacks that climaxed in the Meeker Massacre in Rio Blanco County in 1879. The oldest residents of Colorado, the Utes now live on a small reservation in the southwest corner of the State.

The discovery of gold in the 1850s attracted prospectors and settlers, but mining gold and silver has today largely given way to mining uranium and vanadium, which are used in the State's seven Atomic Energy Commission installations.

Today, historic military posts like Bent's Fort and Fort Garland, once commanded by Kit Carson, contrast with the North American Air Defense Command (NORAD) and the U.S. Air Force Academy, both located near Colorado Springs. Denver, the only mile-high capital and the cultural and business center of the Rocky Mountain region, is the largest city between Texas and California.

Colorado's dry, attractive climate and magnificent scenery may be enjoyed in over a dozen major ski areas, a number of national monuments and national forests, and two national parks—Mesa Verde and Rocky Mountain.

POPULATION	DATE	HISTORIC EVENTS
	1100	Pueblos built cliff dwellings in Mesa Verde
	1540	Coronado believed to have entered area
	1803	Louisiana Purchase brought eastern Colorado to U.S.
		James Purcell, fur trader, first American in area
	1806	Zebulon Pike discovered "Pike's" Peak
	1842	John Fremont explored area
	1848	Part of western Colorado ceded to U.S. by Mexico
	1851	First permanent white settlement at San Luis
	1858	Gold discovered near site of Denver
34,277	1860	
	1861	Became Colorado Territory
	1862	Confederate force from Texas defeated
	1864	Wars with Cheyennes and Arapahoes
39,864	1870	Railroads reach Denver
	1876	Joined Union as 38th State
413,249	1890	
1,035,791	1930	
	1946	Uranium discovered near Grand Junction
1,325,089	1950	First Atomic Energy Commission plant in Colorado—Rocky Flats
	1959	First class graduated from Air Force Academy
2,207.259	1970	

AREA: 104,247 sq. mi.

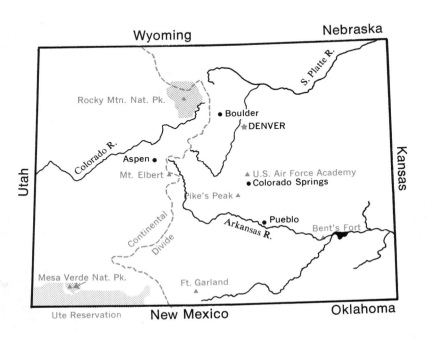

19

CONNECTICUT

(Mohican: "long river place")

*Pequot, Block, Hooker, Fundamental Orders,
Winthrop, Atheneum, Courant, Whitney,
Goodyear, Colt, Nautilus*

Independence, ingenuity, craftsmanship are woven into the fabric of Connecticut's history. In 1639, a century and a half before the Constitutional Convention in Philadelphia, a small group of men met in Hartford and drew up the first constitution to establish a representative form of government. These Fundamental Orders incorporated the principles of Thomas Hooker, the preacher who led colonists from Massachusetts Bay to seek freedom in the wilds of the Connecticut River valley. Independence was also demonstrated by John Winthrop, who in 1657 obtained a charter from Charles II, and by those who hid the charter from the British in the famous "charter oak."

Ingenuity and craftsmanship were demonstrated by the Yankee peddler with his legendary wooden nutmeg; by inventors like Charles Goodyear (vulcanized rubber), Elias Howe (sewing machine), and Eli Whitney (cotton gin); and by such historical firsts as the revolver (Colt), anesthesia (Dr. Wells), and the atomic-powered submarine (Electric Boat Co., Groton).

Connecticut has two great natural gifts: a sheltered shore extending the length of its southern boundary, and the fertile valley of the Connecticut River, which cuts the State in two. The river and the shore form an inverted T that tells much of Connecticut's history. The State's early development centered around its ports—New Haven, New London, Bridgeport, the whaling ports of Mystic and Stonington, and Hartford, the capital, at the head of the tidewater of the Connecticut River, which is now known as the insurance capital of the world. For years Connecticut's coast has been dotted with beaches, resort towns, and scenic villages.

Today, Connecticut ingenuity and craftsmanship continue to be manifest in plants producing tools, clocks and typewriters, as well as guns, sewing machines and complex instruments, but the State's greatest gift to the country—and to the free world—may well be its first: the document that, for the first time in history, dared to make free elections and representative government a reality.

POPULATION	DATE	HISTORIC EVENTS
	1614	Adriaen Block from New Amsterdam discovered Conn.
	1634	First English settlers cam from Massachusetts, founded Wethersfield, Windsor
	1636	Thomas Hooker led over 100 colonists from Massachusetts to found Hartford
	1637	Capt John Mason victorious in Pequot War
	1639	Leaders of Windsor, Wethersfield, Hartford adopted constitution establishing representative govt. (Fundamental Orders)
	1662	John Winthrop, Gov. of Hartford, obtained charter from King Charles II
	1704	Yale college founded
	1764	*Connecticut Courant* first published: oldest newspaper
	1781	Benedict Arnold led British attack on New London
	1784	First American law school established at Litchfield
237,946	1790	
	1795	First insurance company incorporated in Connecticut
	1799	Eli Whitney developed system of manufacturing interchangeable parts
	1807	Noah Webster published first American dictionary
	1835	Colt patented the revolver
	1842	Wadsworth Atheneum, first public art museum, opened at Hartford
	1843	Charles Goodyear developed vulcanizing process
	1844	Dr. Horace Wells of Hartford first used anesthesia
460,147	1860	
908,420	1900	First U.S. Naval submarine built at Groton
1,709,242	1940	
	1954	*Nautilus,* world's first atomic-powered submarine, launched at Groton
2,535,234	1960	
3,032,217	1970	

AREA: 5,009 sq. mi.

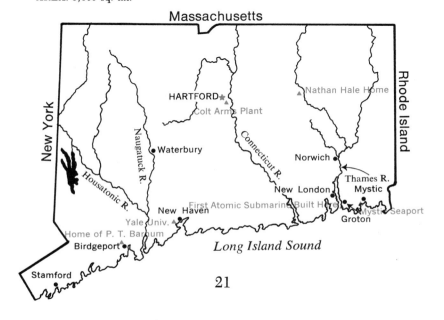

DELAWARE

(After Lord De la Warr)

Leni-Lenape, Hudson, De la Warr,
Zwaanendael, Ft. Christina, Rodney,
Cooch's Bridge, Du Pont, Dickinson

Every four years, representatives of "The First State" lead the President's inaugural parade in Washington, for Delaware was the first of the colonies to ratify the Federal Constitution. And it was one of Delaware's sons—Caesar Rodney—who, in 1776, rode from Dover to Philadelphia to cast the deciding vote in favor of Lee's resolution to declare independence.

The only State whose territory once belonged to Sweden and Holland, Delaware was carved from the giant peninsula that forms Chesapeake Bay. After the English defeated the Dutch, the Duke of York granted the land to William Penn, but Lord Baltimore claimed it as part of Maryland. The dispute was settled only with the establishment of Delaware as a separate State in 1776.

Four thousand men from Delaware fought in the Revolution, but only one small battle (Cooch's Bridge, which the British won) was fought on her soil. British forces also took Wilmington, the capital—which was then moved to Dover.

Although the second smallest State, Delaware has a central location on the eastern seaboard that has fostered the growth of poultry and dairy farms, orchards (apples, peaches) and truck farms, as well as chemical (paints, dyes) and textile (orlon, nylon) industries. The State's favorable tax laws have made it the home of over 44,000 corporations.

In colonial days, the abundance of water power in the north brought mills, and the river and the bay brought shipping and ship building. The State's long coastline permitted development of sport and commercial fishing (oysters, sea trout, crabs); its ocean beaches became popular resorts (Bethany and Rehoboth).

Farms dominate the central and southern sections of Delaware. The industrial and commercial center of the State is Wilmington, one of the chief chemical manufacturing and research centers of the world.

POPULATION	DATE	HISTORIC EVENTS
	1610	Henry Hudson discovered Delaware Bay
	1610	Capt. Samuel Argall of Virginia named bay for Lord De la Warr
	1631	Dutch established first settlement (Zwaanendael) near Lewes
	1638	Peter Minuit established first permanent settlement, Ft. Christina
	1655	Peter Stuyvesant conquered Swedish forts
	1664	English won area from Dutch
	1682	Duke of York granted the territory to Wm. Penn
	1765	Caesar Rodney and Thomas McKean attended Stamp Act Congress
	1776	Delaware completely separated from Pennsylvania
	1777	Sept 3 Battle of Cooch's Bridge—American flag first displayed in battle
	1786	John Dickinson presided over Annapolis Convention (forerunner of Const. Conv.)
	1787	Dec 7 Delaware first State to ratify new constitution
59,096	1790	Delaware ratified 11 of first 12 Amendments to *U. S. Constitution*
	1802	Du Pont powder mill built on Brandywine River
	1829	Chesapeake & Delaware canal completed
112,216	1860	
	1861	Though a slave State, Delaware fought with the Union
223,003	1920	
	1951	Delaware Memorial Bridge opened—connecting Del. and N.J.
548,104	1970	

AREA: 2,057 sq. mi.

23

FLORIDA

(Spanish: "flowery")

Seminole, Ponce de Leon, Menendez,
St. Augustine, Jackson, Everglades,
Palm Beach, Cape Kennedy

The first part of the continental U.S. to be discovered by Europeans, Florida occupies the largest peninsula in the nation—over 400 miles of low, flat land that separates the Atlantic and the Gulf of Mexico.

Florida's rich history, which includes three centuries of Spanish rule, lives in the relics of the original St. Augustine and in tales of French and Spanish explorers. Unlike the other States on the Atlantic coast, Florida was not one of the original thirteen; it became a Territory in 1819, a State in 1845.

Florida's shape, location and climate have greatly influenced its history and development. In the sixteenth century, its location near the treasures of Central America brought Spanish and French explorers and pirates; in the nineteenth, its mild climate stimulated organized farming and experiments with citrus fruits, which became the chief crop; in the twentieth, its 4,000-mile coast, with many harbors, bays and beaches, has attracted increasing numbers of tourists and residents, and the beaches, sailing, and deep-water fishing have made famous such resorts as Miami Beach, Palm Beach, Tampa, and St. Petersburg.

Besides oranges and grapefruit, Florida raises garden crops, peanuts, tobacco and sugar cane. Lumbering, paper mills and dairy farms are found in the north; cattle-raising is concentrated in the south-central section. The processing and canning of frozen foods has become one of the State's major industries.

It is perhaps symbolic that the coast, which has meant so much to Florida, should link together two points that encompass the State's entire history: four centuries but only 120 miles apart are the nation's oldest city (St. Augustine) and the gateway to space at Cape Kennedy.

POPULATION	DATE	HISTORIC EVENTS
	1513	Ponce de Leon explored Florida coast
	1564	French built Ft. Caroline
	1565	Pedro Menendez defeated French and founded St. Augustine, oldest city in U.S.
	1763	Spain ceded Florida to England
	1783	England traded Florida to Spain for Bahamas
	1810	W. Florida declared independent of Spain
	1812	W. Florida became U.S. Territory
	1819	U.S. purchased E. Florida from Spain
34,730	1830	Andrew Jackson, provisional governor, moved Indians to center of Territory
	1835	Seminole War
	1845	Joined Union as 27th State
	1861	Florida seceded, joined Confederacy
	1868	Rejoined Union
187,748	1870	
752,619	1910	
2,771,305	1950	
	1961	First American in space (Cdr Alan Shepherd) launched from Cape Canaveral (now Kennedy)
	1962	First American to orbit earth (Col. John Glenn) launched from Cape Canaveral
	1969	First American to walk on moon (Neil Armstrong) launched from Cape Kennedy
6,789,443	1970	

AREA: 58,560 sq. mi.

25

GEORGIA

(After George II of England)

Cherokee, Creek, DeSoto, Menendez,
Oglethorpe, Suwanee, Chickamauga,
Okefenokee, Stone Mountain, Warm Springs

The Empire State of the South, Georgia has a mild climate, with resorts ranging from ocean beaches to mountain lakes, a balanced economy with plants processing products from its own farms and forests, and a city that has become the commercial center of the Southeast—Atlanta.

The largest State east of the Mississippi, Georgia was founded by English settlers primarily to serve as a buffer between the Carolina colony and the aggressive Spanish in Florida. Named after George II, it was the last of the colonies established by England. The rich soil attracted planters and farmers; large plantations were established, especially in the north-central region, and cotton became the principal crop. It remains so today.

A dark chapter in Georgia's history was the removal of the entire Cherokee nation (17,000 men, women and children) from its ancient tribal lands in northwestern Georgia in 1838. Their tragic "trail of tears" to what is now Oklahoma was marked by indescribable suffering, from which 4,000 died.

Georgia was essentially a farm State until after the Civil War. During Reconstruction, Georgia suffered greater devastation than any other southern State, but, in the last decades of the nineteenth century, new factories and industries helped the State recover. It has become an important producer of textiles, chemicals, processed foods, marble, paper and lumber, and is the world's prime source of turpentine and resins. Besides cotton, its farms grow tobacco, peanuts, hogs and cattle, poultry, pecans and peaches. And its factories and mills use the farm products to produce frozen foods, peanut oil and butter, cotton-seed oil, cloth, and lumber and paper.

Natural wonders in the State include Stone Mountain—a 1600-foot-high mass of solid granite located near Atlanta; Okefenokee Swamp—over 600 square miles of tropical wilds near the Florida border; and the ocean beaches and islands, such as Jekyll and Sea Islands, that attract vacationers year round.

POPULATION	DATE	HISTORIC EVENTS
	1540	DeSoto—first European to visit area
	1566	Pedro Menendez claimed coastal area for Spain
	1733	Gen. James Oglethorpe established first English settlement
	1742	Spanish defeated at Battle of Bloody Marsh
	1753	Became English province
	1788	Fourth State to ratify Constitution and join Union
82,548	1790	
	1793	Eli Whitney invented cotton gin at plantation near Savannah
340,989	1820	
	1838	Cherokees moved from Georgia to western territory
906,185	1850	
	1861	Seceded from the Union
	1863	Confederate victory at Battle of Chickamauga
	1864	Gen. Sherman captured Atlanta and Savannah on his march to the sea
1,184,109	1870	Rejoined Union
	1881	International Cotton Exposition held in Georgia
2,895,832	1920	
	1927	F. D. Roosevelt established foundation for treatment of polio at Warm Springs
3,123,723	1940	
	1945	Pres. Roosevelt died at "Little White House" in Warm Springs
4,589,575	1970	

AREA: 58,876 sq. mi.

27

HAWAII

("homeland")

Cook, Sandwich, Kamehameha,
Liliuokalani, Dole, Diamond Head,
Waikiki, Mauna Loa, Pearl Harbor

Leis, pineapples, tropical beaches and live volcanoes distinguish the nation's only island State. A group of islands extending over 375 miles, Hawaii lies in the Pacific 2400 miles from California. Of its more than twenty islands, there are six principal ones. Most of the smaller islands are not inhabited.

A stupendous accident of nature, the islands were thrust up 15,000 feet from the ocean floor by great underwater volcanic eruptions in a tropical area where the cooling trade winds provide an equable climate throughout the year. The islands are actually a chain of volcanic mountains that, like icebergs, are mostly below the surface.

Two islands dominate the State: Hawaii, the largest, and Oahu, the most populous. Hawaii's 4000 square miles offer great variety—tropical beaches and dense jungles; vast forests, lava wastes, and fertile plantations; the remains of ancient pagan temples; and snow-covered mountains and the world's largest active volcano—Mauna Loa.

The economic, political and cultural center of the State, Oahu is also the prime tourist attraction and, in Honolulu, the capital, has one of the principal ports in the Pacific. Here also are famous Waikiki Beach, Diamond Head (an extinct volcano), and Pearl Harbor. With less than one-tenth of the land area, Oahu has four-fifths of the State's population.

The other large islands—Maui, Kauai, Molokai, and Lanai—have extensive sugar and pineapple plantations, but they remain comparatively undeveloped.

The nation's youngest State is peculiarly American in its people, who have come from many parts of the world to form a unique society where there is no racial majority and people of widely diverse ancestry live in harmony—a spirit which, according to Rev. Abraham Akaka of Honolulu, is the true meaning of Aloha.

POPULATION	DATE	HISTORIC EVENTS
	1778	Capt. James Cook landed at Kauai, named land Sandwich Islands
	1782	King Kamehameha became ruler of island of Hawaii
	1810	Kamehameha united other islands into kingdom
	1826	Capt. Thomas Jones, USN, negotiated treaty with Hawaii
	1843	U.S. recognized independence of Hawaii
	1863	Kamehameha V, last of dynasty, became king
	1874	Kalakaua elected king
	1875	Treaty gave U.S. exclusive use of Pearl Harbor
	1891	King Kalakaua died in San Francisco; succeeded by sister Liliuokalani
	1893	Queen Liliuokalani deposed
	1894	Republic established: S. B. Dole made president
	1898	Hawaii annexed by U.S.
154,001	1900	Became Hawaii Territory; S. B. Dole first governor
	1903	J. B. Dole, cousin of Governor, began successful cultivation of pineapples
	1908	Congress authorized naval base at Pearl Harbor
	1927	First airplane flight from mainland
422,770	1940	
	1941	Dec 7 Japanese attacked Pearl Harbor
	1959	Joined Union as 50th State
769,913	1970	

AREA: 6,423 sq. mi.

*Shoshone, Nez Perce, Kootenai, Couer d'Alene,
Henry, Wyeth, Lake Pend Oreille, William Borah,
Sun Valley, Boise, Snake River, Arco*

Rugged mountains, deep gorges, large lakes, dramatic waterfalls, barren lava fields—all are found in Idaho, known best for its potatoes and the resort center, Sun Valley. Outstanding natural wonders are Crater-of-the-Moon National Monument, with miles of hardened lava and volcanic cinders; Shoshone Falls, higher than Niagara; and Hell's Canyon, the deepest in North America.

Along—and beyond—Idaho's eastern border stands a wall of mountains, part of the Continental Divide, that protects the State from the severe winters that sweep the plains to the east. From these mountains westward, flow the State's great rivers—Clearwater, Salmon, and Snake. With the help of irrigation, farmers grow grains, fruits, sugar beets and the famous potatoes on the broad valley of the Snake River. Cattle and sheep ranches and dairy farms are also found in the lowlands.

From Idaho's mountains come timber (over 20 million acres of evergreens) and minerals (zinc, copper, gold), and more lead and silver than is produced in any other State. In the north, near Coeur d'Alene, is the nation's largest silver mine. Extensive forests and thousands of lakes and streams provide tourists and sportsmen ample opportunities for recreation.

Several thousand Indians live on State reservations—members of the Kootenai, Nez Perce, Couer d'Alene, Shoshone and Paiute tribes.

The country's thirteenth largest State, Idaho is one of the ten smallest in population. Boise, the capital, is the largest city. Rich in land, timber, minerals and water, Idaho offers almost unlimited space and natural beauty.

POPULATION	DATE	HISTORIC EVENTS
	1805	Lewis and Clark, first white men in area
	1809	British Northwest Co. built first structure, on shore of Lake Pend Oreille
	1810	Andrew Henry of Missouri Fur Co. erected building on Snake River; first by American west of Continental Divide
	1811	Wilson Hunt expedition pioneered Oregon Trail
	1812	British took control of region
	1842	Father Desmet established mission among Couer d'Alenes
	1846	Wm. Craig established first homestead Treaty with England gave U.S. possession below 49th parallel
	1860	Mormons made first permanent settlement, at Franklin Capt. E. D. Pierce discovered gold at Orofino Creek
	1866	Snake War—against Indian tribes in south
14,999	1870	
	1882	Northern Pacific R.R. completed across Idaho
	1889	Constitution adopted
88,548	1890	Joined Union as 43rd State
445,032	1930	
	1951	Atomic energy first used to produce electricity, at Arco
713,008	1970	

AREA: 83,557 sq. mi.

31

ILLINOIS

(Algonquian: "man")

*Illini, Algonquian, Black Hawk, Joliet,
LaSalle, George Rogers Clark, Nauvoo,
Lincoln, Columbian Exposition, Chicago*

"Hog Butcher for the World, Tool Maker, Stacker of Wheat," Carl Sandburg called Chicago in 1914, and the nation's second-largest city is still the number one livestock market and meatpacking center, and the home of many industries and the grain exchange. Before the air age, Chicago became the world's greatest railroad center, and it remains so today; its O'Hare Field is the world's largest commercial airport.

Other, smaller cities—Rockford, Peoria, Springfield, East St. Louis, Elgin—help make Illinois one of the top manufacturing States, with products ranging from locomotives to watches. But the Prairie State, one of the most level in the Union, is farm country: almost 90 per cent of its land is used for farming. In most sections, one sees the ordered fields of corn, wheat, or soybeans, or dairy farms, or farms raising hogs or cattle. The State is one of the top producers of soybeans and corn.

The first groups of permanent settlers came to Illinois from Kentucky and the Carolinas, some with slaves. The central and northern sections were settled largely by pioneers from the northeastern States, and, at the time Illinois joined the Union, the northern boundary was moved far enough north to permit a port on Lake Michigan (Chicago), so that commerce and communication could be maintained with the northern and middle States. This was done so that the entire State would not have to look south, to the Mississippi and Ohio Rivers, for its trade routes. But even at that time, when Illinois joined the Union as a free State, it had several thousand slaves, and slavery remained a critical issue within the State when Douglas defeated Lincoln in 1858—when Lincoln lost the election for U.S. Senator but won the national fame that helped him become Illinois' only President.

Illinois' location, its fertile lands, its rich mineral deposits (large bituminous coal reserves), and its great variety of industries all contribute to make it the Empire State of the Midwest.

POPULATION	DATE	HISTORIC EVENTS
	1673	Joliet and Marquette explored area
	1720	French founded Kaskaskia and Ft. Chartres
	1763	French ceded Illinois lands to Britain
	1774	Became part of province of Quebec
	1778	George R. Clark captured Kaskaskia
	1787	Became part of Northwest Territory
	1809	Became Illinois Territory
12,282	1810	
	1818	Joined Union as 21st State
	1832	Black Hawk War: Indians defeated, driven from State
	1839	Mormons founded Nauvoo
476,183	1840	
	1846	Mormons driven from Illinois
	1848	New constitution abolished slavery
1,711,951	1860	Lincoln elected 16th U.S. President
	1871	Great Chicago Fire
	1893	World's Columbian Exposition held at Chicago
4,821,550	1900	
	1933	Century of Progress Exposition held at Chicago
7,897,241	1940	
11,113,976	1970	

AREA: 56,400 sq. mi.

INDIANA

("land of the Indians")

*Miami, Wea, LaSalle, Vincennes,
George Rogers Clark, Wayne, Harrison,
Tecumseh, French Lick, Indianapolis 500*

The Indianapolis 500—the annual Memorial Day auto race—tells much about Indiana, past and present. The name of the capital—"city of the land of the Indians"—recalls the frontier past, and the 500-mile race, one of the most celebrated national sports events, reflects the State's position as a leader in the automobile world.

During its early history, Indiana was indeed the "land of the Indians": even when it entered the Union, over half the State was held by Indians. The Indian wars made General William H. Harrison famous, and his victory at Tippecanoe gave him his campaign slogan ("Tippecanoe and Tyler, Too") when he ran for President in 1840.

Since the beginning of this century, automobiles have been built in the South Bend area. Other important products are iron and steel (Gary), machinery (Ft. Wayne), musical instruments (Elkhart), refrigerators (Evansville), and books and chemicals (Indianapolis). The Bedford quarries are a major source of building stone, the mines in the southwest a rich producer of bituminous coal. Gas and oil, clay and gypsum are other valuable resources.

Most of the State is prairie with rich farmlands that produce corn, rye, wheat, soybeans, spearmint and peppermint, and on which are raised hogs and cattle. Fruit and tobacco are grown in the hilly area near the Ohio River.

Small lakes formed by glaciers abound in the North, man-made lakes in the South, which also boasts such natural features as huge caves (Wyandotte cave is second largest in the U.S.) and mineral springs (French Lick and West Baden).

Indianapolis, the capital and largest city, lies near the center of the State. In 1820, commissioners selected this location, even though the site was then a dense forest. Today over half a million people live there—in the nation's second largest city not on navigable waters.

34

POPULATION	DATE	HISTORIC EVENTS
	1679	LaSalle first white man in area
	1732	French established first permanent settlement at Vincennes
	1779	George Rogers Clark captured Vincennes from British
	1784	First American settlement at Clarksville
	1794	Gen. Anthony Wayne defeated Indians at Fallen Timbers
	1795	Twelve Indian tribes ceded part of area to U.S.
5,641	1800	Became Indiana Territory
	1806	First general assembly met at Vincennes
	1811	Gen. Harrison defeated Tecumseh at Tippecanoe
	1813	Capital moved to Corydon
	1816	Joined Union as 19th State, with strong anti-slavery Constitution
	1825	Capital moved to Indianapolis
685,866	1840	
	1846	National Road completed across Indiana
	1851	New constitution adopted
1,350,428	1860	
2,192,404	1890	
	1894	Elwood Haynes built America's first spark-ignition auto at Kokomo
3,427,796	1940	
5,193,669	1970	

AREA: 36,291 sq. mi.

IOWA

(Sioux: "beautiful land")

Sauk, Fox, Ioway, Sipus,
Potawatomi, Marquette, DuBuque,
Ft. Madison, Herbert Hoover, Cedar Rapids

Iowa is Farm Country, U.S.A., with 97 per cent of its land cultivated. One of the wealthiest farm States, it has long been a leading source of corn, oats, soybeans and hay, as well as hogs and cattle, poultry and dairy products. Exceptionally rich soil—combined with the use of improved fertilizers, seeds and equipment—has made Iowa farms models of scientific farming. In 1959, Soviet Premier Khrushchev visited a large modern farm near Cedar Rapids.

Until the 1830s, members of the Sauk, Fox, Ioway, Sipus, Winnebago, Potawatomi and other tribes occupied the area, but by 1850, the Federal Government had moved most of them to "Indian Territory"—what later became Oklahoma, and settlers had already discovered the unusual growing power of Iowa's exceptionally rich soil. By the 1870s, Iowa had enough farmers to join Illinois and Minnesota as leaders of the Granger Movement (the forerunner of the Grange)—fighting for laws to protect the farmers from exploitation and misuse of power by the rapidly expanding railroads and by owners of grain elevators.

Today, with well over 100,000 farms, Iowa in some years supplies as much as one-tenth of the country's food. In crop value, Iowa generally ranks second to California. Farm-related industries have assumed an important place in Iowa's economy, and Des Moines, Davenport, Cedar Rapids, Council Bluffs and Waterloo produce farm machinery, tools and fertilizers. Some of these also produce flour and cereals: the breakfast cereal mill in Cedar Rapids is the largest in the world.

Several Iowa cities have become major centers of insurance: over fifty insurance companies have their home offices in the State. But the State which lies between the Mississippi and Missouri rivers, near the middle of the continent, which is also the middle State in size (25th),—the State which gave the nation its thirty-first President, Herbert Hoover, is best known as "the land where the tall corn grows."

POPULATION	DATE	HISTORIC EVENTS
	1673	Joliet and Marquette explored area
	1762	French ceded area to Spain
	1788	Julien DuBuque opened lead mine
	1800	Spain ceded area to France
	1803	France sold area to U.S., part of Louisiana Purchase
	1804	Lewis and Clark explored parts of Iowa
	1812	Indians drove Americans from first settlement at Ft. Madison
	1830	Dr. Isaac Galland built first school—in Lee County
	1838	Became Iowa Territory
	1839	Capital moved from Burlington to Iowa City
43,112	1840	
	1846	Joined Union as 29th State
	1856	Iowa's first railroad built: Davenport to Iowa City
	1857	Capital moved from Iowa City to Des Moines
		Last Indian hostilities: Sioux attacked Spirit Lake settlement
	1858	John Brown fled through Iowa with 25 slaves
674,913	1860	
1,624,615	1880	
	1928	Herbert Hoover elected 31st U.S. President
2,470,939	1930	
	1959	Premier Khrushchev of USSR visited Garst farm
2,825,041	1970	

AREA: 56,290 sq. mi.

37

KANSAS

(Sioux: "South-wind people")

*Kansa, Osage, Wichita, Pawnee, Comanche,
Apache, Coronado, Pike, Becknell, Dodge City,
Carry Nation, Hugoton, Eisenhower*

Geodetic center of the continent and geographic center of the 48 contiguous States, Kansas has for centuries been the hub of major travel routes. The network of Indian trails that Coronado and his men found in the Kansas prairie in 1541 did not distract them from their search for the City of Gold, but these later became the Chisholm, Sante Fe, and Oregon Trails, and the routes of the Pony Express and the railroads—the paths that brought civilization to Kansas and beyond, and made Kansas the crossroads of the West.

Kansas did not undergo change without turmoil. In gaining statehood, Kansas endured its own civil war years before the Civil War began. The Kansas-Nebraska Act left it to the citizens of these new territories to decide if either would be slave or free. After this Act was passed, in 1854, both abolitionists and pro-slavery forces swarmed into Kansas, and raids and killings brought "bleeding Kansas" to national attention. Both pro-slavery and free constitutions were prepared—and contested—before Kansas finally entered the Union as a free State.

With the railroads came rapid growth. From Texas, huge cattle herds were driven to "cow towns" on the railroad like Abiline and Dodge City, and farmers were lured by the railroad's offers of cheap land. Mennonites from Russia brought to the fertile prairie the hardy Red Turkey wheat seed—the germ of what is now the nation's largest wheat crop. Other crops—corn, soybeans and rye—and huge cattle ranches, have made agriculture for many years Kansas' principal industry.

In the past thirty years manufacturing has become increasingly important—with products ranging from farm equipment to airplanes: over half the private aircraft built in the world are made in Wichita, the largest city.

The State is also a rich source of minerals—oil, coal, gypsum and helium, plus the world's largest known gas fields (at Hugoton), and the world's greatest salt deposits (at Hutchinson).

Modern Kansas has an enviable record for developing programs for health and welfare, and the Menninger Foundation in Topeka is world renown for its contributions to mental health.

POPULATION	DATE	HISTORIC EVENTS
	1541	Coronado explored western Kansas
	1719	French explorer Claude du Tisne crossed southwestern Kansas
	1803	French sold area to U.S., part of Louisiana Purchase
	1804	Lewis & Clark explored area
	1806	Lt. Zebulon Pike made treaties with Kansa and Osage Indians
	1821	William Becknell pioneered Sante Fe Trail across Kansas
	1854	Kansas-Nebraska Act established Territory of Kansas
	1855	Pawnee made capital
107,206	1860	First railroad in Kansas—from Elwood to Wathene
	1861	Joined Union as 34th State—a Free State
	1863	Quantrill's Confederate force attack Lawrence
		Kansas St. Univ. established—first land-grant college
	1867	U.S. officials signed treaties with Indians at Medicine Lodge, home of Carry Nation, anti-liquor crusader
	1872	Dodge City founded—"Queen of the Cow Towns"
996,096	1880	State passed law prohibiting sale of liquor
	1887	Mrs. Medora Salter became first woman mayor in world
1,428,108	1890	
	1948	Repeal of law prohibiting sale of liquor
1,905,299	1950	
	1953	Dwight Eisenhower from Abilene elected 34th U.S. President
2,249,071	1970	

AREA: 82,276 sq. mi.

KENTUCKY

(Wyandotte: "meadowland")

15th

Wyandotte, Walker, Harrod, Boone,
Bourbon, McGuffey, Lincoln, Davis,
Kentucky Derby, Mammoth Cave

Wedged between the Ohio River and the Appalachian Mountains, Kentucky holds a special place in American history: the first western State, it represented the beginning of the thrust westward that was ultimately to transform the collection of coastal States into a continental nation. This has given epic significance to the journey of that first group of settlers which Daniel Boone led through the Cumberland Gap into the wilderness beyond the mountains. Soon after, others came to the area—either through the Gap or down the Ohio River.

Sheltered in crude log cabins, the first settlers grew hemp and tobacco, and raised hogs and cattle—and horses. Pioneers from Virginia, Maryland and the Carolinas brought Thoroughbred horses to the blue-grass pastures around present Lexington—now the nation's leading Thorough-bred breeding region.

Kentucky played a difficult role in the Civil War: both Lincoln and Jefferson Davis, President of the Confederacy, were born in Kentucky, and the State had divided interests and allegiances, but it remained with the Union.

Through the years Kentucky has become most famous for bourbon whiskey, Thoroughbred horses, the great store of U.S. Government gold at Fort Knox, and Mammoth Cave—one of the Seven Natural Wonders of the modern world. And, at Churchill Downs, near Louisville, each year the finest horses in the world compete in the Kentucky Derby.

On Kentucky's farms, tobacco remains an important crop; cigaret making, meat packing, leather tanning, and the manufacture of farm machinery and electrical equipment are prominent industries. Minerals include coal, oil and cement.

The mountains and the Ohio River, which shaped Kentucky's early history, have in the twentieth century become more valuable for recreation, but history has left its mark in the paths of the pioneers through the mountains and in the river cities of Covington, Paducah and Louisville.

POPULATION	DATE	HISTORIC EVENTS
	1750	Thomas Walker discovered Cumberland Gap
	1769	Boone explored area extensively
	1774	James Harrod established first permanent settlement west of Appalachians, Harrodsburg
	1775	Boone established Boonesboro
	1776	Virginia Assembly created Kentucky County
	1787	*Kentucky Gazette* first published: first newspaper west of Alleghenies
	1789	Elijah Craig, a Baptist minister in Bourbon County, made first bourbon whiskey
73,677	1790	
	1792	Joined Union as 15th State
	1794	Legislature authorized free public schools—first in U.S.
	1798	Legislature adopted Kentucky Resolutions: proposed nullifying Alien and Sedition Acts
220,955	1800	
	1823	William McGuffey produced first *McGuffey Reader,* while teaching near Paris
687,917	1830	
	1833	Legislature passed law prohibiting sale of slaves
1,115,684	1860	Native son Abraham Lincoln elected 16th U.S. President
	1861	Native son Jefferson Davis elected President of Confederacy
	1875	First Kentucky Derby
2,147,174	1900	
	1936	Mammoth Cave made national park
2,845,627	1940	
3,219,311	1970	

AREA: 40,395 sq. mi.

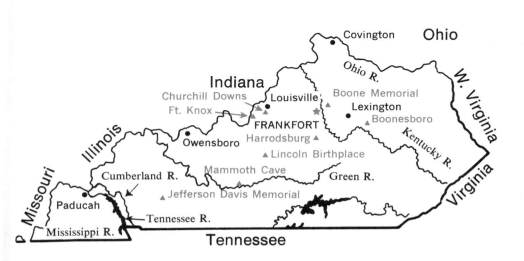

LOUISIANA

(After Louis XIV of France)

Acolapissa, Atakapa, Natchez, DeSoto,
Nathchitoches, Creole, Bienville,
Acadians, Chalmette, Mardi Gras

Louisiane was what the French called the vast area of the Mississippi River basin that Napoleon sold to the U.S. in 1803, in the largest single territorial acquisition in American history, and the Gulf Coast section that is now Louisiana was the cultural heart of the Territory. The French who settled there in the seventeenth and eighteenth centuries left a rich heritage: the French—and Creole—language, customs, laws (derived from the Code Napoleon), foods and ornamented houses with courtyards make modern Louisiana the most French of all States.

New Orleans—the State's largest, most distinctive city—reflects its French heritage in the *Vieux Carre* (Old French Quarter), the annual Mardi Gras celebration, and the famous Creole restaurants. Known as the birthplace of American jazz, the city still boasts some of the finest jazz musicians.

With the help of slaves, early settlers in Louisiana established large plantations and grew sugar and cotton, which, with rice, remain its leading crops. Coastal waters yield oysters, shrimp and fish; the Delta marshes provide muskrat fur for women's coats. The State ranks with the top four or five in the production of oil, has thriving lumber and paper industries, and a growing number of chemical plants.

The first State to join the Union out of the original Louisiana Territory, Louisiana can claim the most varied history of any State: its lands (divided into "parishes") and its waterways ("bayous") have been under eight different flags—French *Fleur de Lis,* and the flags of Spain, Britain, Napoleon, the Republic of West Florida, the Republic of Louisiana, the Confederacy, and the U.S., and the State retains much of the flavor of the 120 years under the Spanish and French flags.

POPULATION	DATE	HISTORIC EVENTS
	1543	DeSoto's men descended Mississippi
	1682	LaSalle claimed Mississippi River Basin, and named it, for Louis XIV
	1714	First permenent settlement, at Natchitoches
	1718	de Bienville founded New Orleans
	1760-90	Acadians moved from Nova Scotia to Louisiana
	1762	France ceded land to Spain
	1763	Treaty of Paris gave U.S. area east of Miss.
	1800	Spain ceded land to France
	1803	U.S. bought Louisiana Terr. from France
76,556	1810	Eastern lands became Republic of W. Florida
	1812	Joined Union as 18th State
	1815	Jan 8—Gen. Jackson defeated British at Chalmette, near New Orleans
	1838	First Mardi Gras
352,411	1840	
	1861	Seceded from Union; was independent republic for six weeks
726,915	1870	
1,381,625	1900	
	1901	First oil well in State—near Jennings
2,363,880	1940	
	1964	Federal courts ordered integration of schools in New Orleans, other cities
3,643,180	1970	

AREA: 48,523 sq. mi.

MAINE

(After ancient French province)

Algonkin, Norsemen, Smith,
Battle of Margaretta, Aroostook,
Longfellow, Moosehead Lake, Mt. Katahdin

The farm, the sea, and the forest—emblazoned on the seal—tell the story of the State of Maine: the nation's potato bin, a leader in shipbuilding and fishing with a long, picturesque coast, and an important producer of paper and lumber.

The most northeasterly section of the country, Maine was in the path of early explorers. Over 25,000 Algonkins were living in semi-permanent villages along the principal rivers when the first colonists came, and they resisted the white settlers for almost 200 years. The first settlements were built along the low coastal lands; even today the mountainous, heavily wooded interior remains sparsely settled. Fishing and the building of ships occupied the early settlers; they later built whalers and sleek clipper ships, sailing those speedy vessels to distant oceans. And fishermen discovered the cod, tuna and shellfish (lobsters, crabs, and clams) that, with sardines, still come from Maine today.

For over 300 years, lumbering—including wood products—has been Maine's chief industry. Falls in its rivers provided power for sawmills, and the lumber, pulp, and paper industries have continued to grow with the State, which has an active reforestation program. More famous, perhaps, is its potato crop, the nation's largest. Most are grown in Aroostook County in the north. Important also are blueberries, apples, poultry, and dairy products. And Maine is an important manufacturer of shoes.

From Maine have come such famous citizens as Commander Robert E. Peary, the explorer; writers Artemus Ward and Sarah Orne Jewett; and Henry W. Longfellow.

Maine is indeed "Vacationland," with snow-country winter sports; cool summers; immense forests of pine, fir and spruce; over 2,000 lakes (including Moosehead Lake—largest in New England); many mountains (Mt. Katahdin—5627 ft.); an abundance of rivers and streams; and a rugged and varied coastline of 2400 miles with numberless beaches, harbors, coves and islands.

THE PINE TREE STATE

POPULATION	DATE	HISTORIC EVENTS
	1000	Vikings believed to have reached Maine coast
	1524	Verrazano explored coast
	1604	French founded colony on St. Croix River
	1607	Plymouth Co. founded colony on Kennebec River; lasted one year
	1614	John Smith explored and mapped coast
	1623	First permanent settlement, on Saco River
	1652	Maine became part of Massachusetts
	1675	Beginning of Indian wars
	1775	First naval engagement of Revolution, Battle of Margaretta, off coast at Machais
96,540	1790	
298,335	1820	Joined Union as 23rd State: part of Missouri Compromise
	1838	Aroostook War—border conflict with British
501,793	1840	
	1842	Webster-Ashburton Treaty settled border dispute
	1846	Legislature passed law prohibiting sale of liquor
	1854	Clipper ship *Red Jacket,* built at Rockland, made record run—New York to Portland
626,915	1870	
	1872	First Federal fish hatchery established at Bucksport
768,014	1920	
	1934	Prohibition of liquor repealed
847,226	1940	
993,663	1970	

AREA: 33,215 sq. mi.

45

(After Queen Henrietta Maria of England)

*Susquehannas, Smith, Calvert, Religious
Toleration Act, Francis Scott Key, Antietam,
Naval Academy, Goddard Space Center*

The nation's largest bay—the Chesapeake—separates Maryland's mainland from the Eastern Shore, and it has been the center of Maryland life for over three centuries. Early colonists, drawn by the promised religious toleration of the Catholic Lord Baltimore, settled the fertile coastal lands, which they cleared to plant tobacco. The bay and its contributing rivers provided easy routes for trade and an unlimited source of seafood. Today thousands of commercial fishermen and sportsmen seek the bay's nearly 300 species of fish and shellfish. Maryland clams and crabcakes have long been world famous.

Marylanders have made unique and dramatic contributions to U.S. history. Near the end of the Revolution, in the critical days before the Articles of Confederation were adopted, Maryland delegates played a leading role in forcing Virginia, New York, Massachusetts and Connecticut to relinquish claims to the territory west of the Ohio River, actions which led to the creation of the first territory from which new States could ultimately be formed. And names like Francis Scott Key and Barbara Fritchie have long since passed into legend.

As in colonial days, cattle and dairy farms are tucked in the folds of the rolling hills and mountains of central and western Maryland. Colonists found virgin forests covering 90 per cent of the State; now about half the land is wooded. The lowlands of the Eastern Shore, always suited to farming, produce garden vegetables—especially tomatoes—and poultry. This land, part of the Delmarva (parts of Del., Mar. and Va.) Peninsula, has an Atlantic port and fine sea beach at Ocean City.

Most of Maryland's population is concentrated in two areas—Baltimore and the suburbs of Washington—which have almost become one. One of the largest cities in the U.S., Baltimore is a world port and the industrial, commercial and cultural center of the State. To the south, at the mouth of the Severn River, is Annapolis, the capital, with the U.S. Naval Academy, the wooden-domed State House, and well-preserved houses and buildings that help the city retain the charm of colonial America.

POPULATION	DATE	HISTORIC EVENTS
	1608	John Smith explored Maryland coast
	1632	Charles I granted the land to Lord Baltimore (Cecil Calvert)
	1634	Leonard Calvert, Cecil's brother, arrived with 200 settlers
	1638	The legislature won right to initiate laws
	1649	Religious Toleration Act passed
	1652	Susquehannas ceded territory to Maryland
	1767	Penn.-Md. line set by British mathematicians Mason and Dixon
	1781	Maryland ratified Articles of Confederation
	1783-7	Annapolis made capital of thirteen States under Confederation
	1783	Continental Congress ratified Treaty of Paris, ending Revolution
	1786	Meeting in Annapolis led to Constitutional Convention
	1788	Joined Union as 7th State
319,728	**1790**	
	1791	Maryland ceded land for District of Columbia to Federal Govt.
	1814	Francis Scott Key of Frederick composed *Star Spangled Banner* when Ft. McHenry survived British bombardment
447,040	**1830**	
	1845	U.S. Naval Academy opened
687,049	**1860**	
	1862	Gen. McClellan's troops defeated Confederate forces near Antietam
1,188,044	**1900**	
1,821,244	**1940**	
	1961	Goddard Space Center established
3,922,399	**1970**	

AREA: 10,577 sq. mi.

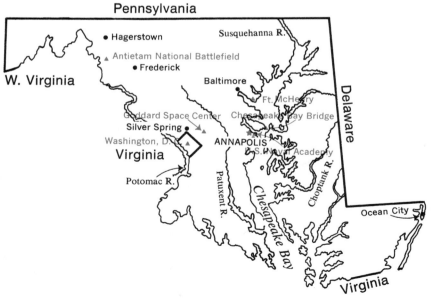

47

MASSACHUSETTS

(Indian: "large hill place")

Gosnold, Smith, Mayflower, Harvard,
Salem, Lexington, Adams, Revere, Hancock,
Thoreau, Emerson, Hawthorne, Cape Cod, JFK

First of the northern colonies in America, Massachusetts gave birth to the American Revolution, but her founding was a monumental accident of history. Destined for Virginia, where they held grants, the Mayflower Pilgrims were driven north by storms and sought refuge in Plymouth Harbor. With no rights to the land, they drew up the Mayflower Compact, an action that fate had forced upon them.

Besides majority rule and the town meeting, the Pilgrims established the first tax-supported schools, the first college, and the first library in the Colonies.

It is a paradox that this State was, in the 17th century, an intolerant theocracy which banished free-thinkers and hanged "witches," and, in the 18th, became a leader in the move for independence. Samuel Adams, Paul Revere and John Hancock lead the list of patriots—and the colony strongly supported the Revolution with men and supplies.

Rocky, thin soil turned early settlers to fishing and shipbuilding, and later to operating small factories and mills. Modern Massachusetts leads in the manufacture of shoes and leather goods, and, in the Boston-Cambridge area, has a growing electrinics and research center.

Natural attractions include the Berkshire mountains in the west; thousands of lakes and ponds; picturesque fishing villages; the resort islands of Martha's Vineyard and Nantucket; and Cape Cod, the crescent of sand on which are found Provincetown, Barnstable, and Hyannisport—home of President John F. Kennedy.

A leader in education and the arts since colonial times, Massachusetts gave America a distinctive literature, which was created by Thoreau, Emerson, Hawthorne, Poe and others. This century has seen development of outstanding music and dance festivals in the Berkshires, and a distinguished theater group at Provincetown. Harvard, M.I.T., Radcliffe, Smith and Wellesley have long been at the forefront of American education—and all but Smith are close to Boston, which has for three centuries been the Hub of New England—its history, industry and culture.

POPULATION	DATE	HISTORIC EVENTS
	1602	Bartholomew Gosnold visited Massachusetts Bay & named Cape Cod
	1614	John Smith explored coast, named New England
	1620	Mayflower landed at Plymouth
	1630	Gov. Winthrop and 1,000 arrived
	1636	Roger Williams banished from colony
		Harvard College founded—first in America
	1644	Colony persecuted Baptists and Quakers
	1691-2	Witchcraft trials, executions, in Salem
	1765	Samuel Adams led resistance to Stamp Act
	1770	March 5—Five colonists killed in uprising, called "Boston Massacre"
	1773	Boston Tea Party
	1775	Apr. 19 Colonists defeated British at Lexington & Concord
		June 17 Colonists victorious at Bunker Hill
	1788	First cotton mill established at Beverly
		Joined Union as 6th State
378,787	1790	
	1796	John Adams elected 2nd U.S. President
	1824	John Q. Adams elected 6th U.S. President
610,408	1830	
	1832	First society against slavery formed
1,457,351	1870	
3,366,416	1910	
4,316,721	1940	
	1960	John F. Kennedy elected 35th U.S. President
	1963	Pres. Kennedy assassinated in Texas—youngest martyred Pres.
5,689,170	1970	

AREA: 8,257 sq. mi.

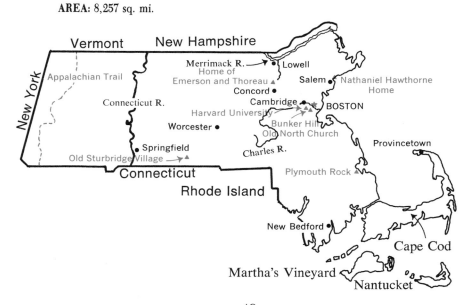

MICHIGAN

(Chippewa: "greak lake")

*Michilimackinac, Chippewa, Ottawa,
Marquette, Cadillac, Grand Rapids,
Negaunee, Jackson, Ford*

The Indians named the area *michi gama* ("great lake"), and Michigan is the only State to border on four of the five Great Lakes. It is also the only State made from two peninsulas—which are now joined by the Mackinac Bridge, one of the world's longest suspension bridges.

Several hundred years ago, the Chippewas and Ottawas who hunted in the forests and fished on the lakes of both peninsulas saw fur trappers, and then traders and settlers move into these attractive lands. The waterways provided transportation and, in the 1800s, Greak Lakes' steamboats brought large numbers of settlers.

Lumbering was, for a time, the principal industry—as were copper and iron mining—and the variety of hardwoods found in the rich forests supplied the raw materials for cabinet- and carriage-makers. It was the tradition of skilled carriage-makers, coupled with the success of small shops making motors for boats, that provided conditions favorable to the development of the first horseless carriages. Out of the first small automobile shops has grown one of the world's largest industries and the world's largest corporation, with headquarters in Detroit.

Construction of the canal at Sault. St. Marie provided an outlet from Lake Superior that proved invaluable for shipping iron ore to the more southerly Great Lakes ports.

The growth of the automobile, furniture and other industries—such as household appliances, the discovery of iron ore in the northern peninsula, and the increased number of fruit farms on the eastern shore of Lake Michigan, have not reduced the natural attractions of the State, and the many beaches, lakes and forests of Michigan are each year sought by thousands of sportsmen and vacationers.

THE WOLVERINE STATE

POPULATION	DATE	HISTORIC EVENTS
	1618	Etienne Brule first white man in area
	1641	Jesuits Charles Raymbault and Isaac Jogues visited Chippewas
	1668	Pere Marquette founded first permanent settlement, Sault St. Marie
	1701	Antoine Cadillac founded Detroit
	1715	French built Ft. Michilimackinac
	1760	British seized Michigan settlements
	1767	Pontiac, chief of Ottawas, attacked Detroit
	1783	British ceded Michigan lands to U.S.
	1787	Area included in Northwest Territory
	1805	Became Michigan Territory
4,762	1810	
	1818	First Great Lakes steamboat landed at Detroit
	1837	Joined Union as 26th State
212,267	1840	
	1844	Iron ore deposits discovered at Negaunee
	1854	Republican Party formed at mass meeting at Jackson
	1855	Canal at Sault St. Marie opened
1,184,059	1870	
2,093,890	1890	
	1892	Henry Ford built first automobile in Detroit
4,842,325	1930	
	1933	Closing of banks in Michigan precipitated national crisis
6,371,766	1950	
8,875,083	1970	

AREA: 58,216 sq. mi.

51

MINNESOTA

(Sioux: "sky-colored water")

Ojibway, Sioux, Radisson, DuLuth,
St. Anthony Falls, Grange, Mesabi,
Lindbergh, Mayo, Guthrie

Minnesota is indeed "The Land of Sky-Blue Waters." Over 4,000 square miles of water are in this comparatively level State that is laced with rivers and thousands of lakes. Here also are the sources of three great continental river systems: The Rainy and Red Rivers go north to Hudson Bay; the St. Louis and Pigeon Rivers go east to Lake Superior and the St. Lawrence; and from Lake Itasca, a narrow stream winds south to become the Mississippi.

Vikings may have visited this land and fought with the Indians, but the source of this information—the Kensington Rune Stone—is believed by some scholors to be a hoax.

After the Sioux and Ojibway gave up their lands in the 1850s, there was a rush of settlers who turned to lumbering, farming—raising primarily wheat—and building and operating flour mills on the waterways. With the aid of the railroads, which reached Minnesota in the 1870s, and of lumberjacks like the fabled Paul Bunyan, the virgin timber was cut and shipped to eastern markets—and uncontrolled exploitation drastically reduced the supply. By the early 1900s Minnesota had become the greatest iron-ore-producing State, and it now produces fifty million tons a year, 60 per cent of the nation's total. Most ore from the Mesabi and Vermilion ranges is shipped from Duluth in Great Lakes freighters to steel plants in Chicago and Gary, and the Cleveland-Youngstown area.

Until recently, farming was the State's leading industry: second only to Wisconsin in dairy production, Minnesota also produces wheat, corn, soybeans and flaxseed, as well as livestock and poultry (it ranks second in raising turkeys).

Manufacturing has become Minnesota's principal industry, ranging from meat-packing and flour-milling to producing machinery and electrical equipment. Many industries are located near the twin cities—Minneapolis and St. Paul, the cultural center of the State, with a nationally known symphony orchestra and center for the arts, the Tyrone Guthrie Theater. To the south, in Rochester, is the world-famous Mayo Clinic.

POPULATION	DATE	HISTORIC EVENTS
	1659	Radisson and Chouart first white men in area
	1679	DuLuth claimed land for King Louis XIV of France
	1763	French ceded land east of Mississippi to England
	1783	British ceded lands to U.S.
	1803	Louisiana Purchase brought western Minn. to U.S.
	1805	Lt. Pike took over posts still held by British
	1820	Ft. St. Anthony established near present Minneapolis
	1832	Schoolcraft discovered Lake Itasca, source of Mississippi
	1837	Ojibway and Sioux ceded lands between Mississippi and St. Croix Rivers
	1849	Became Minnesota Territory
6,077	1850	
	1851	Sioux ceded lands west of Mississippi
	1854	Ojibway ceded northern lands
	1858	Joined Union as 32nd State
	1867	Oliver Kelley of Elk River founded National Grange
439,706	1870	Edmond La Croix invented flour purifier in Minneapolis mill
	1884	First ore mined on Vermilion Range
1,310,183	1890	Discovery of Mesabi Range—world's largest iron ore deposits
2,387,125	1920	
	1927	Charles Lindbergh of Little Falls first to fly non-stop New York to Paris
3,805,069	1970	

AREA: 84,068 sq. mi.

MISSISSIPPI

(Choctaw: "father of waters")

Chickasaw, Choctaw, Seminole, Natchez,
DeSoto, LaSalle, d'Iberville,
Eastern Star, Vicksburg, King Cotton

The fertile soil and low flat lands, ample rainfall and warm climate, make Mississippi an ideal area for raising cotton, and for over a century it has been the State's leading crop. When the first planters, with the help of slaves, laid out the large plantations, tobacco and indigo were the principal crops, but after the invention of the cotton gin, cotton quickly became number one.

Like Georgia and Alabama, Mississippi included lands that had for centuries been held by the Civilized Tribes, Indians known for their printed alphabet and developed culture. In the 1830s—in violation of long-standing Federal treaties—the entire Choctaw and Chickasaw nations were forcibly moved from their lands to Arkansas and Oklahoma Territories.

In the nineteenth century, steamboat traffic on the Mississippi River developed the ports of Vicksburg and Natchez, both prominent in the State's history. Vicksburg was the scene of a critical battle of the Civil War; General Grant said that the Union victory there "sealed the fate of the Confederacy." Natchez has one of the largest collections of classic antebellum mansions in the South.

Along Mississippi's Gulf coast are thriving fisheries and canneries: it is the nation's prime source of shrimp and oysters. The canneries' whistles signal arrival of the shrimp boats, calling the workers immediately to pack the fresh shrimp.

A diversification program has introduced such crops as corn, oats, wheat and soybeans to Mississippi. The Chinese tung tree yields valuable oil for paints and varnishes, and the State ranks first in the growth of hardwood timber. In the southern section are most of Mississippi's lumber and paper mills. The State has also become an important source of oil and gas. These varied industries contribute significantly to the State's economy and its growth in this century, but Mississippi's unique character still derives largely from the great river, from King Cotton, and from its many monuments and enduring symbols of the Old South.

THE MAGNOLIA STATE

POPULATION	DATE	HISTORIC EVENTS
	1541	DeSoto discovered Mississippi River
	1542	DeSoto died near Natchez, buried in river
	1682	LaSalle explored area, named Louisiana
	1699	d'Iberville established settlement on coast
	1763	France ceded area to Britain
	1798	Became Mississippi Territory
7,600	1800	
	1814	Treaty of Ft. Jackson: Indians ceded lands
	1817	Joined Union as 20th State
75,448	1820	
	1831-7	Choctaw and Chickasaw moved to western lands
606,526	1850	Rob Morris founded Eastern Star in Jackson
	1861	Seceded from the Union
	1863	Battle of Vicksburg
	1865	End of war in Mississippi; surrender of General Taylor
	1869	Rejoined the Union
827,922	1870	
1,790,618	1920	
	1939	Oil discovered at Tinsley
	1962	James Meredith, first Negro admitted to U. of Mississippi
2,216,912	1970	

AREA: 47,716 sq. mi.

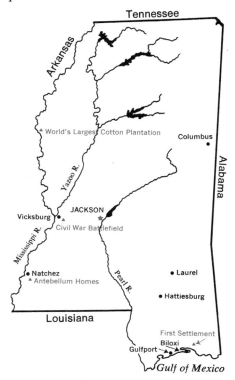

MISSOURI

(Algonquian: "canoe haver")

Osage, Sac, Fox, Oto, Missouri,
Miami, Lewis & Clark, Liguest,
Twain, Pershing, Truman, Saarinen Arch

Through Mark Twain the world learned of life in a small Missouri town on the Mississippi River in the mid-nineteenth century—a time when the open plains were becoming farmland, when the towns of Franklin and Westport were starting points for the Sante Fe Trail, and when riverboats were making St. Louis a mid-continental port.

With settlers from both northern and southern States, Missouri was from the beginning caught up in the slavery question: as part of the Missouri Compromise, it entered the Union as a slave State, but future States from north of its southern boundary were to be free. Yet, in the Civil War, Missouri stayed with the Union.

Today, as in the nineteenth century, over half of Missouri is farm land —producing livestock, corn, soybeans, cotton, and dairy products. For over fifty years the State has been one of the nation's prime sources of lead, and it is the home of a growing aerospace industry. Kansas City is a leader in the processing and preparation of foods.

Along the riverfront in St. Louis stands Saarinen's Gateway Arch, the tallest national monument, which symbolizes the role of Missouri's largest city as the Gateway to the West. Named after King Louis of France, St. Louis was once the capital of Upper Louisiana. It has long been the regional business and cultural center—America's largest producer of beer, second to Detroit as a maker of automobiles and to Chicago as a rail center. Its museums and theaters, its symphony (second oldest in the U.S.), its architecture, and its wealth of historic sites—like Forest Park, scene of the 1904 World's Fair—mark it as a metropolis of the Midwest.

POPULATION	DATE	HISTORIC EVENTS
	1682	LaSalle claimed area for France
	1735	French established first permanent settlement, St. Genevieve
	1762	France ceded area to Spain
	1764	Pierre Liguest founded St. Louis
	1802	Spain ceded area to France
	1803	Bought from France as part of Louisana Purchase
	1804	Lewis & Clark expedition left St. Louis to explore Louisiana Ter.
19,783	1810	
	1812	Became Missouri Territory
	1821	Joined Union as 24th State
	1828	Sen. Thomas Benton sought gradual emancipation of slaves
383,702	1840	Peak of buffalo hunting: American Fur Co. sold 67,000 pelts
	1846	Dred Scott case challenged constitutionality of Missouri Compromise
	1847	Legislature established penalties for teaching Negroes
1,721,295	1870	
	1874	Eads Bridge at St. Louis dedicated: first across Mississippi River
	1876	Twain's *Adventures of Tom Sawyer* published
	1884	Twain's *Adventures of Huckleberry Finn* published
3,106,665	1900	
	1917	Gen. John Pershing, of Laclede, led A.E.F. in World War I
3,784,664	1940	
	1945	Harry Truman became 33rd U.S. President
4,677,399	1970	

AREA: 69,674 sq. mi.

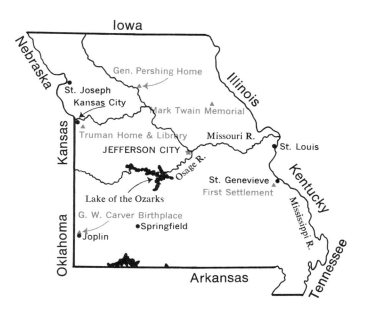

MONTANA
(Latin: "mountainous")

41st

Blackfoot, Crow, Sioux, Kootenai, Cheyenne,
Verendrye, Little Big Horn, Arder Gulch,
Butte, Glacier National Park, Fort Peck Dam

The majestic purple mountains that gave Montana its name are not its only treasures: it also has rich deposits of copper, zinc, gold and silver; extensive oil fields; and fine farm and grazing lands. On its plains are 10,000-acre cattle and sheep ranches and farms that grow wheat, barley and sugarbeets—some by irrigation; in its west are the towering forested mountains of the Continental Divide. Near the Canadian border are the spectacular peaks, waterfalls and glaciers of Glacier National Park.

The discovery of gold in the mountains brought the first settlers (1850s and 1860s), but significant growth came only after peace was made with the Indians (1877) and the railroad lines reached the State (1880s). One of the last—and most dramatic—battles with the Indians was the tragic encounter at the Little Big Horn, when General Custer and his men were killed by Sioux and Cheyenne warriors. A century later, over five million of the State's 100 million acres are Indian lands, where more than half of Montana's 31,000 Indians live. The Ft. Peck Reservation, settled by Assiniboine and Sioux, has proved a valuable source of oil, and most of the 2,000 oil and gas leases on Montana's Indian lands are found there.

Although gold was the first mineral discovered in Montana, silver and copper gradually replaced it in importance. Montana is now a leading producer of oil, copper and zinc, and it has at Butte one of the world's largest copper mines, but the many huge farms and ranches make agriculture number one in the State.

Forests cover one quarter of Montana, with over half in its eleven national parks. These forests provide lumber and, with the lakes, streams and other natural wonders in wilderness areas, offer endless opportunities for sports and recreation.

POPULATION	DATE	HISTORIC EVENTS
	1743	Pierre de la Verendrye first white man to explore area
	1803	Eastern Montana bought by U.S. in Louisiana Purchase
	1805	Lewis and Clark first Americans to explore area
	1807	Manuel Lisa built first trading post, on Big Horn River
	1829	American Fur Co. established Ft. Union near Missouri River
	1841	Father De Smet founded St. Mary's mission, first permanent settlement
	1852	Francois Finlay discovered gold in Deer Lodge valley
	1863	Rich gold deposits discovered at Alder Gulch
	1864	Became Montana Territory
	1866	First cattle driven from Texas to Montana
20,595	1870	
	1876	Gen. Custer and over 200 soldiers killed at Little Big Horn by Sioux & Cheyenne
	1883	North Pacific railroad completed across Montana
	1889	Joined Union as 41st State
142,924	1890	
	1913	Natural gas discovered near Glendive
	1915	Oil discovered at Elk Basin
548,889	1920	
559,456	1940	Ft. Peck Dam on Missouri River completed; largest earth-filled dam in world
	1953	Hungry Horse Dam on Flathead River completed
694,409	1970	

AREA: 147,138 sq. mi.

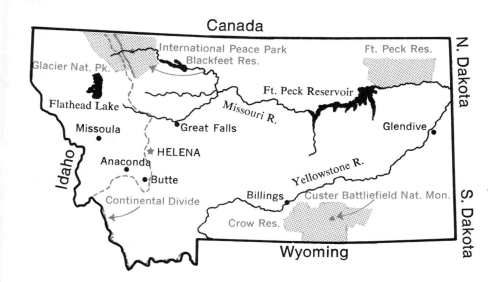

NEBRASKA

(Omaha: "flat river")

Pawnee, Omaha, Otoe, Ponca, Sioux,
Arapahoe, Winnebago, Bellevue,
Overland Trail, Homestead, Morton

This midwestern State has the nation's only unicameral (one-house) legislature and a 400-foot-tall capitol that does *not* resemble the Capitol in Washington. Like Mississippi, Connecticut and other States, Nebraska took its name from the Indian name for its principal river (the Omahas called it *Nibthaska*, the Otoes *Nibrathka*—both meaning "flat river"), but, unlike the other States, it then changed the name of the river—to the Platte (French for "flat"). And flat—and treeless—was most of this land when pioneers reached it, but a sustained tree-planting program, led by J. Sterling Morton, founder of Arbor Day, has created a man-made National Forest that now covers over 24,000 acres.

Nebraska is the home of Willa Cather, celebrated novelist of the West; William Jennings Bryan, three times a Presidential candidate; and Senator George Norris, the father of public power and TVA. At North Platte is Scout's Rest Ranch, the home of "Buffalo Bill" Cody.

A large underground water reserve helps Nebraska raise the wheat, corn, alfalfa, cattle and hogs that are its chief products. Nearly three million acres are irrigated. Extensive cattle raising and dairy farming have made Omaha a major cattle market and packing center. Food processing, based on the State's agriculture, is its largest industry, but it also produces a variety of goods—from electrical equipment to mobile homes.

Thousands of pioneers passed through Nebraska along the Overland Trail to California, and, before Congress passed the Homestead Act in 1862, few remained on the treeless prairie where the Pawnee, Omaha, Sioux and Cheyenne roamed freely. Later, homesteaders staked out their 160 acres, built sod huts, and those in the eastern and southern sections discovered that they had exceptionally fertile, easily tillable soil. The western hills and high plains proved best for raising cattle. Near the town of Beatrice is the first farm ever claimed under the Federal act that offered free land almost for the taking.

POPULATION	DATE	HISTORIC EVENTS
	1795	French traders built post in northeast Nebraska
	1823	French built Bellevue on Missouri R.; first permanent settlement
	1824	Trading post established at present Omaha
	1841	First Oregon-bound settlers passed through Platte River valley
	1847	Brigham Young led Mormons through Nebraska
	1854	Became Nebraska Territory; Omaha made capital
		May 30 Kansas-Nebraska Bill signed by President Pierce—
		left open the question of slavery
	1855	Gen. Harney's U.S. troops attacked Sioux village at Blue Water Creek
28,841	1860	Pony Express used Overland Trail through Nebraska
	1862	First homestead in nation claimed by Daniel Freeman, near Beatrice
	1863	Union Pacific railroad reached Omaha
	1867	Joined Union as 37th State; capital moved to Lincoln
	1872	J. Sterling Morton founded Arbor Day
	1876	U.S. Fifth Cavalry drove 800 Cheyenne & Sioux to reservations
452,402	1880	
1,062,656	1890	
1,377,963	1930	
	1937	Unicameral system, with 43 senators, adopted
1,483,791	1970	

AREA: 77,047 sq. mi.

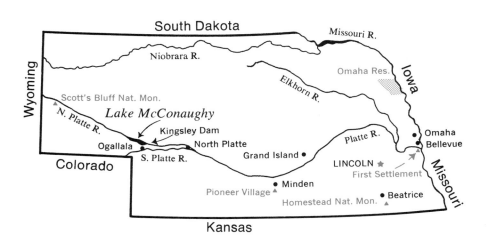

NEVADA

(Spanish: "snow-clad")

36th

Paiute, Mohave, Bannock, Washoe,
Fremont, Comstock Lode, Virginia City,
Hoover Dam, Lake Mead, Las Vegas

Range after range of mountains and endless stretches of desert kept the early pioneers from the Nevada country. A few trappers and explorers came in the early 1800s, and the Gold Rush to California (1849), which brought thousands through the State, created several trading posts and small settlements, but it was the discovery of silver deposits in 1859 that brought the first surge of people—and prosperity—to Nevada.

By 1900 many gold and silver mines were exhausted, but in the years since, other minerals have been discovered—manganese, mercury, tungsten, lead, zinc and copper. After 1900, irrigation helped develop farmland; and ranching, with great herds of cattle and sheep grazing on Federal lands, has become an important part of Nevada life. But the State that lies in the Great Basin, where streams from the mountains sink and disappear, the State with less rain than any other, brought people and prosperity in the twentieth century by legalizing gambling and establishing comparatively easy divorce laws. The millions of visitors to Las Vegas and Reno now provide over half of the State's income.

One of the largest States (7th), Nevada remains one of the smallest in permanent population. Carson City is the smallest State capital in the U.S.

Besides the striking mountains and brightly flowered desert, Nevada has such other natural attractions as Lake Tahoe, the amazingly beautiful Lehman Caves, and Death Valley; and such man-made wonders as the near ghost-town of Virginia City, Lake Mead, and Hoover Dam—the highest in the Western Hemisphere.

POPULATION	DATE	HISTORIC EVENTS
	1825	Ogden discovered Humboldt River
	1827	Jediah Smith crossed Nevada
	1833	Bonneville pioneered route later used by railroad
	1841	First emigrant train crossed area to California
	1843	Fremont explored region
	1848	Became part of U.S. (Washoe County of California)
	1849	Mormons established one of first settlements, at Genoa
	1850	Became part of Utah Territory
	1858	Carson City founded
	1859	Comstock Lode—one of world's richest metal deposits—discovered
6,857	1860	
	1861	Became Nevada Territory
	1864	Joined Union as 36th State
42,335	1900	
	1904	Copper ore discovered at Ely
81,875	1910	
91,058	1930	
	1931	Gambling legalized and divorce requirements reduced
	1936	Hoover Dam completed
160,083	1950	
488,738	1970	

AREA: 110,540 sq. mi.

63

NEW HAMPSHIRE

(After Hampshire County, England)

Champlain, Mason, Thompson, Andros,
Stark, Dartmouth, Webster, Pierce,
Franconia Notch, Mt. Washington

In January of 1776, six months before the Declaration of Independence was signed, New Hampshire's congress formally declared its independence, and the State has maintained a tradition as the home of sturdy men and women of independent spirit—qualities captured by Stephen Vincent Benet in his story "The Devil and Daniel Webster." New Hampshire was the ninth—and deciding—State to ratify the Federal Constitution: its action assured the formation of the new republic.

Captain John Mason, who was granted the New Hampshire land and is considered the State's founder, named it after his native county in England. The first colonists, many from Massachusetts, settled along the 19-mile coast and turned to fishing. Later, colonists opened the wooded coastal plain and the valleys of the Merrimack and Connecticut rivers, creating the farms that until the 1800s were the primary source of income, and developing the lumbering industry that remains important today. Over 80 per cent of the State is covered with forests.

Some of the first factories in America appeared in New Hampshire, when small workshops and mills were built along the rivers, which provided power and easy transportation. Textiles and clothes, shoes, pulp and paper were produced. In Manchester was Amoskeag Mill—largest textile mill in the world. In recent years New Hampshire has added industries producing electrical equipment and machinery.

Besides timber—and maple sugar—New Hampshire's natural resources include feldspar, mica and granite. Its quarries have provided the stone for many of the nation's monuments and public buildings, including the Library of Congress in Washington. At Franconia Notch is the natural rock profile featured in Hawthorne's "The Great Stone Face." Other natural attractions are the ocean beaches, Lake Winnipesaukee, and the White Mountains, with Mt. Washington, at 6,288 feet, the highest peak in New England.

POPULATION	DATE	HISTORIC EVENTS
	1605	Champlain discovered Isles of Shoals
	1622	First land grants to John Mason, founder of N.H.
	1623	David Thompson established first settlement at Little Harbor
	1630	Laconia Co. colonists settled at Portsmouth
	1640	Boundary disputes with Massachusetts
	1679	New Hampshire established as separate province
	1686	Became part of Dominion of New England, under Sir Edmund Andros
	1756	N.H. *Gazette* founded—oldest continuously published paper in U.S.
	1776	Jan 15 First assembly of provincial congress declared independence
	1777	Aug 16 Gen. Stark of New Hampshire defeated British at Bennington
	1788	June 17 Ninth State to ratify Constitution
141,885	1790	
	1819	Dartmouth College Case: Supreme Court ruled that N.H. could not make Dartmouth a State college; established inviolability of a contract
284,574	1840	
	1852	Franklin Pierce of Hillsboro elected 14th U.S. President
411,588	1900	
491,524	1940	
	1957	Restoration of Portsmouth's historic Strawberry Banke begun
737,681	1970	

AREA: 9,304 sq. mi.

Canada

Connecticut R.

Mt. Washington
(6,288 Ft.)

Franconia Notch

Vermont

Appalachian Trail

Maine

Lake Winnipesaukee

Merrimack R.

Piscataqua R.

Franklin Pierce Home

CONCORD

Strawberry Banke
(Restored Village)

Hillsboro

Portsmouth

Manchester

Atlantic Ocean

Nashua

Massachusetts

NEW JERSEY

(After island of Jersey)

Lenni Lenape, Hudson, Berkeley, Carteret,
Westminster Treaty, Battle of Princeton,
Edison, Palisades, Atlantic City

Standing between two of the nation's greatest cities—New York and Philadelphia—New Jersey is one of the principal industrial States. Its many industries—from chemical and medicine plants to copper and oil refineries—are concentrated in a narrow strip between these two cities, extending from Passaic and Paterson to Trenton and Camden.

Northwest of this industrial belt, in the only highlands in the State, are dairy and poultry farms and the Delaware Water Gap, a deep gorge cut through the Kittatinny Mountains. Along the Hudson River, across from New York City, stand the sheer cliffs of The Palisades. To the south, on the coastal plain, are farms that grow fruits and vegetables—the "garden" crops that give the State its nickname. The Atlantic coast, with over 100 miles of sandy beaches, is dotted with vacation resorts; best known is Atlantic City, with its boardwalk and annual Miss America contest.

During the American Revolution, nearly 100 battles were fought in New Jersey—including the Battle of Trenton, won by Washington after he and his troops made the historic crossing of the Delaware River on Christmas night 1776. Throughout the State, Revolutionary battle sites are preserved as historic shrines.

Menlo Park, near Plainfield, is the research laboratory in which Thomas Edison developed many of his over-1000 inventions. In the State today are many modern chemical research laboratories.

Because of its central location, as well as its favorable laws governing corporations, New Jersey has attracted a great variety of industries and businesses. Over 15,000 factories within its borders supply this densely populated State and the neighboring States that, together, make up the most thickly settled area in the United States.

POPULATION	DATE	HISTORIC EVENTS
	1524	Verrazano landed on New Jersey coast
	1609	Henry Hudson sailed up Hudson River, claimed land for Dutch
	1614	Cornelius May explored Delaware River
	1664	Charles II granted brother James, Duke of York, Dutch holdings, including New Jersey
		James granted N.J. to Berkeley and Carteret
	1673	Dutch regained control of area
	1674	Treaty of Westminster gave English control of New Jersey
	1676	Quakers bought western half of New Jersey from Berkeley
	1702	New Jersey became royal province
	1746	College of New Jersey (later Princeton) founded
	1776	Washington crossed Delaware River, Christmas night
	1777	Battle of Princeton
	1786	Delegates from New Jersey attended Annapolis Convention
	1787	New Jersey delegates at Constitutional Convention sponsored "small-State" plan
		Dec 3 N.J. third State to ratify Constitution
184,139	1790	
	1794	First factory—calico-printing shop—built at Paterson
373,306	1840	
	1844	New constitution abolished property qualifications for voting
1,444,933	1890	
3,155,900	1920	
4,835,329	1950	
6,066,782	1960	
	1967	Extensive riots in Newark
7,168,164	1970	

AREA: 8,219 sq. mi.

Pennsylvania
New York
Delaware Water Gap
Patterson
George Washington Bridge
Hudson R.
Newark
Jersey City
Elizabeth
Thos. Edison Laboratory
Menlo Park
Princeton University
Princeton
TRENTON
Delaware R.
Camden
Delaware
Atlantic City

NEW MEXICO

47th

(Spaniards' name for area)

Sandia, Folsom, Pueblo, Navajo, Vaca,
Coronado, Onate, Sante Fe, Gadsden,
Los Alamos, Carlsbad Caverns, Gallup Indian Ceremonial

Eighty years before the Pilgrims landed at Plymouth Rock, Coronado and his men visited the land of the Pueblos, bringing horses for the first time into what was to be U.S. territory. Later, cattle and sheep were brought by Spanish colonists—the first cattlemen of the West, and by 1610 the Spaniards had built the Palace of the Governors, which still stands—the oldest public building in the U.S.

For centuries the Pueblos had lived—as many still do—in apartment-like adobe structures, some terraced on the face of cliffs. A peaceful people who raised corn and beans and made glazed pottery, the Pueblos resisted the Spaniards, and today on their reservations many still follow practices of their ancient culture.

The influence of both the Spaniards and the Pueblos can be found in New Mexico's modern cities and towns, where Spanish names and customs abound, and Indian-made pottery, rugs, paintings and silver jewelry are sold. Some of these towns sprang up after the Sante Fe Trail was pioneered in the 1820s.

Early settlers farmed and raised livestock. In this century, the construction of Elephant Butte Dam and Navajo Dam created large areas of new farmland—land devoted primarily to cotton, the principal crop.

Minerals found in New Mexico include uranium, oil, copper, zinc, and potash. The nation's greatest source of uranium ore, New Mexico has, since World War II, become a center for atomic research.

A land of contrasts, New Mexico boasts White Sands desert and forested mountains, endless plains and massive mesas and buttes, deep canyons and fertile fields—and Carlsbad Caverns, a natural wonder that includes the largest underground room in the world.

Besides its sizeable Indian population, most of whom live in eighteen pueblos and four reservations, New Mexico each August is host to tribes from all North America at the Inter-Tribal Indial Ceremonial, held near Gallup. There, members of many tribes compete for prizes in arts and crafts, dancing and riding—at the largest annual Indian celebration in the U.S.

68

POPULATION	DATE	HISTORIC EVENTS
	1530	Cabeza de Vaca explored area; returned to Mexico with tales of golden cities
	1540	Coronado searched area for golden cities
	1598	Juan de Onate founded San Gabriel, first European settlement
	1610	Sante Fe founded; made capital
	1680	Pueblos revolted; drove out Spanish
	1692	Spanish troops regained control
	1821	First caravan left Missouri for Sante Fe
		Became part of Republic of Mexico
	1846	Became part of U.S.
61,547	1850	Became New Mexico Territory
	1853	Gadsden Purchase: acquired border area from Mexico
	1868	Navajos placed on reservations
119,565	1880	Apaches placed on reservations
327,301	1910	
	1912	Joined Union as 47th State
531,818	1940	
	1942	Manhattan Project started at Los Alamos
	1945	July 16 World's first nuclear weapon detonated near Carrizozo
	1962	Navajo Dam built
1,016,000	1970	

AREA: 121,666 sq. mi.

69

NEW YORK

(After Duke of York, later James II)

Algonquin, Mohawk, Cayuga, Hudson, Stuyvesant,
Nicolle, Erie Canal, Irving, Whitman, Melville,
Niagara, Empire State Building, Roosevelt

The largest city in the western hemisphere and the trade capital of the world is the cornerstone of what George Washington called "The Empire State." The first capital of the U.S., New York City has since become the undisputed financial, commercial and cultural center of the nation. Its trade and shipping, stock exchanges, libraries, museums, theaters, galleries, restaurants and night clubs—and the United Nations headquarters—make it one of the world's greatest cities—bought, it is reported, for $25 worth of trinkets.

All of New York State was not so easily bought: there were wars in the Hudson valley with the Algonquins and, in central New York, with the Indian Confederacy (Mohawk, Oneida, Onandaga, Cayuga and Seneca).

New York State extends from its great ocean port across the Appalachians to a prime Great Lakes port—Buffalo; and these two ports and the route between them—through the Hudson and Mohawk valleys—tell much of the story of the Empire State. As the nation moved westward, the lowland route to the Great Lakes became increasingly important: in 1825 the Erie Canal linked the Hudson River and Lake Erie; soon after, the main lines of the railroad were built along the Hudson-Mohawk lowlands, connecting New York City with Chicago and the West. Along this route sprang up the State's main manufacturing cities—Troy, Schenectady, Utica, Syracuse and Rochester—and its capital, Albany. From 1820 until the 1960s, New York was the nation's most populous State.

North of the Mohawk Valley are the lakes and forests of the Adirondack mountains; to the south, most of the State's poultry and dairy farms. There are vineyards in the west, orchards along the Hudson valley. Overlooking the Hudson is the U.S. Military Academy, at West Point, and, not far away, Hyde Park, the home of Franklin Roosevelt.

From the Empire State came the two Roosevelts, and some of America's most distinguished writers—Washington Irving, James Fenimore Cooper, Walt Whitman, and Herman Melville.

POPULATION	DATE	HISTORIC EVENTS
	1609	Henry Hudson explored the Hudson River
		Samuel Champlain explored northern lakes
	1623	Dutch established first permanent settlement, Ft. Orange
	1626	Peter Minuit purchased Manhattan from Indians
	1647	Peter Stuyvesant made governor
	1664	British Col. Nicolle seized area
	1754	Colonial Congress met in Albany
	1774	N.Y. Assembly proposed calling Continental Congress
	1776	Apr 13 Washington arrived in N.Y. to prepare for attack
		Sept 15 Gen. Howe took N.Y.
	1786	Treaty of Hartford—Massachusetts gave up claims to western N.Y.
	1788	Joined Union as 11th State
	1789	New York City made temporary U.S. capital
340,120	1790	
1,372,812	1820	
	1825	Erie Canal opened
	1836	Martin Van Buren elected 8th U.S. President
3,097,394	1850	
6,003,174	1890	
	1901	Theodore Roosevelt became 26th U.S. President
10,385,227	1920	
12,588,066	1930	
	1932	Franklin Roosevelt elected 32nd U.S. President
14,830,192	1950	
16,782,304	1960	
	1964	New York World's Fair
18,190,740	1970	

AREA: 49,576 sq. mi.

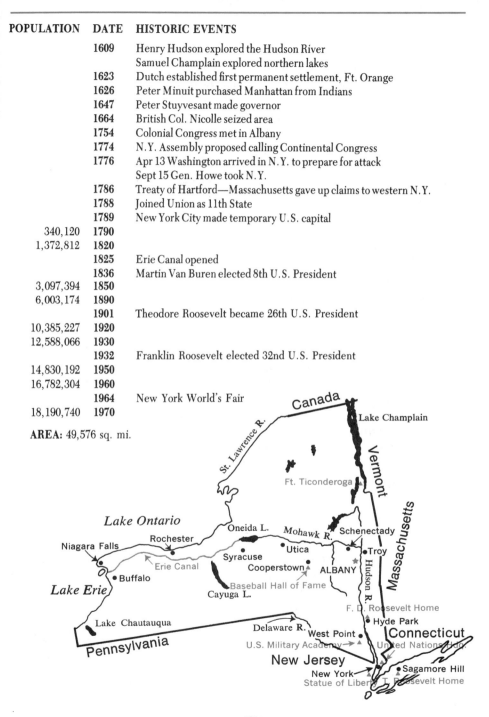

71

NORTH CAROLINA 12th

(After Charles II of England)

Croatan, Cherokee, Muskogean, Roanoke
Island, Virginia Dare, Blackbeard,
Tarheel, Mecklenberg, Hatteras, Kitty Hawk

The first English settlement in North America was on Roanoke Island, the still unexplained "Lost Colony" of 150 settlers who—with Virginia Dare, the first child of English parents born in America—vanished between 1587 and 1590. Later, around 1650, settlers from the Jamestown area of Virginia moved into northern Carolina and established the first permanent settlements.

A year before the celebrated Boston Tea Party, a group of Carolina women protested British injustices in an act known as the Edonton Tea Party. And in May 1775—over a year before the 13 colonies signed the famous Declaration of Independence—a group of citizens in Mecklenberg County adopted resolutions declaring their independence from British rule.

Reluctant to leave the Union in 1861, North Carolina was one of the last States to secede, but she gave more men to the Confederate cause than any other State.

A unique feature of North Carolina is its Outer Banks, a string of islands that protects much of the mainland from the open sea. These strips of land have been the scene of dramatic events: the vanishing of the Lost Colony—pirates such as Capt Kidd and Blackbeard (Edward Teach) burying stolen treasure—thousands of ships sinking off stormy Cape Hatteras—and the Wright brothers soaring in man's first powered flight. Part of the area is now preserved as a national seashore.

Today, the State's coastal plain and piedmont region grow more tobacco than does any other State. At Winston-Salem and Durham are the world's largest cigaret factories; also at Winston-Salem is Old Salem, a restored early American village. This region's rivers—the Neuse, Cape Fear, Yadkin, and Catawba—provide the hydroelectric power for the nation's largest collection of textile mills. Lumbering and furniture making are found throughout the State, with lumbering the principal enterprise in the western mountains. In the Blue Ridge Mountains are Great Smoky National Park, almost 800 square miles of untouched forest, and Mt. Mitchell, eastern America's highest peak.

POPULATION	DATE	HISTORIC EVENTS
	1524	Verrazano explored coast
	1585	Lane and Grenville established first English colony on Roanoke Island; later, colonists vanished
	1587	Aug 18—Virginia Dare, first English child born in America
	1663	Charles II of England granted territory to eight proprietors
	1669	Proprietors adopted constitution written by John Locke
	1677	Culpeper's Rebellion—against Navigation Act: first rebellion against foreign rule in America
	1711	Indians defeated in Tuscarora War
	1712	North Carolina established as separate province
	1718	Pirate Edward Teach ("Blackbeard") killed at Ocracoke
	1729	North Carolina became royal colony
	1775	May 31 Mecklenberg Resolutions adopted; established government independent of King
	1780	British defeated at King's Mountain
	1781	Cornwallis victorious at battle of Guilford Courthouse
	1789	Convention at Fayetteville ratified U.S. Constitution
393,751	1790	
753,419	1840	
	1861	May 20—Seceded from the Union
1,617,949	1890	
	1903	Wright brothers flew first powered aircraft—at Kitty Hawk
	1908	Prohibition adopted
3,170,276	1930	
5,082,059	1970	

AREA: 52,712 sq. mi.

NORTH DAKOTA

(Sioux: "allies")

Hidatsa, Sioux, Mandan, Chippewa, Assiniboine,
Verendrye, Pembina, Nicollet, Fremont,
Theodore Roosevelt, Badlands, Garrison Dam

Long before Columbus, bands of Vikings are believed to have visited the North Dakota area, coming up the Red River of the North, the only northern-flowing river in the U.S. If they did, they might have seen the Mandan Indians, a friendly tribe reported by early trappers to be successful farmers and skilled artisans, a tribe destroyed almost overnight by a smallpox epidemic in 1837.

The land of such other tribes as the Arikara and Hidatsa saw French explorers come from Canada, and American fur traders and early settlers come up the Missouri. Immigration increased after Dakota Territory was formed and land was made available for homesteading (obtaining public land free by cultivating it and living on it). The northern climate attracted many Scandinavians, most of whom endured the kind of hardships depicted in Rolvaag's *Giants in the Earth.*

From pioneer days, wheat has been the principal crop, and North Dakota is now second only to Kansas in total wheat production; in hard spring wheat and durum wheat—as well as flax and rye—it leads the nation. Cattle ranches are found mainly in the western prairie, dairy farms in the Red River valley. The contruction of Garrison Dam across the Missouri River, with its 200-mile-long lake, added thousands of acres to North Dakota's farm and ranch lands. In recent years, profitable oil fields have been discovered in the northwest, and lignite—brown coal—is mined in the north and central sections.

North Dakota has a variety of unusual attractions: Theodore Roosevelt National Memorial Park is located in the Badlands. For two years Dakota Territory was the home of Roosevelt: the cabin in which he lived is now on the grounds of the capitol. In the Turtle Mountains on the Canadian border is the International Peace Garden, a symbol of enduring friendship. And at Rugby, in the north-central section, is a stone cairn marking the geographical center of North America.

POPULATION	DATE	HISTORIC EVENTS
	1682	La Salle claimed part of N.D.
	1738	Pierre de la Verendrye, first white man to enter N.D., visited Mandan Indians
	1762	France ceded land to Spain
	1800	Spain ceded American possessions to France
	1803	Louisiana Purchase brought southwestern N.D. to U.S.
	1804-5	Lewis & Clark crossed N.D.
	1812	First permanent white settlement established at Pembina
	1818	Treaty of Paris (with British) fixed northern boundary at 49th Parallel
	1839	John Fremont and Jean Nicollet led first exploration through central N.D.
	1861	Became Dakota Territory
	1863	Dakota Territory opened for homesteading
2,405	1870	Treaty with Chippewa & Sioux brought peace in eastern area
36,909	1880	
	1881	Northern Pacific R.R. completed line through Dakota Terr.
	1883	Territorial capital moved from Yankton to Bismarck
	1889	Nov 2, N.D. joined Union, with S.D., as 39th & 40th States
190,983	1890	
319,146	1900	
577,056	1910	
	1951	Oil discovered near Tioga
	1953	Garrison Dam completed
617,761	1970	

AREA: 70,665 sq. mi.

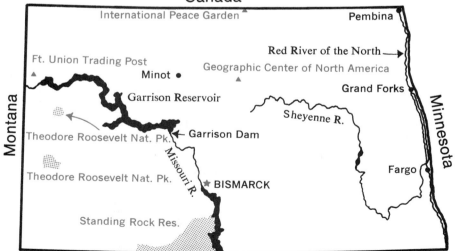

OHIO

(Indian: "great")

Iroquois, Miami, Erie, LaSalle, Marietta,
Northwest Ordinance, Treaty of Green Ville,
Moses Cleaveland, Perry, Glenn

The first of the organized territories to be carved from the Northwest Territory, Ohio was also one of the first to begin the process of becoming a State that was to be followed so many times as the nation expanded westward. The process had been clearly defined in the Northwest Ordinance.

Modern Ohio divides naturally into three sections: the North, with the ports of Toledo and Cleveland, where the New England heritage is greatest; the South, dominated by the river and Cincinnati; and the heartland, where farms and small cities surround the capital.

Although small (35th), Ohio is populous (6th), ranking high in both manufacturing (3rd) and farming (12th). Two-thirds of its people live in cities, which include one of the world's greatest producers of rubber (Akron), and the largest iron-ore port (Cleveland). It has forty-three colleges and universities, more than every State except Pennsylvania.

Ohio has proved true to its Indian name: "great." Its greatness derives from its resources, its location, and its people. It has unusual natural gifts—fertile rolling land with numerous lakes and rivers; rich deposits of clay, coal and gas; and a strategic location just west of the Appalachians between Lake Erie and the Ohio River.

During the eighteenth century, the Iroquois, Eries, Miamis, Wyandottes and Ottawas fought the French, the English, and the new Americans, as well as each other, for Ohio lands. Military campaigns and treaties gradually removed the Indians.

As part of the Northwest Territory, the region was one of the first to experience the westward movement after the Revolutionary War. First settlers came from the Eastern Seaboard—from New England to Virginia. As the country grew, canals, highways and railroads made Ohio an important link with the West. And, with the coming of steel, Ohio found itself, with fine lake ports, located between the iron ore ranges of Minnesota and the coal fields of Pennsylvania and West Virginia.

Ohio's people represent many nationalities; the State early achieved a diversity that made it a typical American melting pot. From these people have come such distinguished Americans as Edison and the Wright brothers and seven U.S. Presidents.

POPULATION	DATE	HISTORIC EVENTS
	1669	La Salle explored area
	1749	George II chartered first Ohio Company
	1752	George Washington explored Ohio River Valley
	1772	Moravians founded first village, Schoenbrunn
	1774	Became part of Britain's Quebec Province
	1787	Northwest Ordinance established
	1788	First permanent settlement at Marietta
	1795	Treaty of Green Ville: Indians ceded eastern Ohio
	1796	Moses Cleaveland founded Cleveland
	1799	Northwest Territory organized
45,365	1800	
	1803	Joined Union as 17th State
	1813	Sept 10 Commodore Perry defeated British on Lake Erie
	1816	Columbus made capital
581,434	1820	
3,198,062	1880	James Garfield elected 20th U.S. President
4,157,545	1900	William McKinley re-elected 25th U.S. President
5,759,394	1920	Warren Harding elected 29th U.S. President
7,946,627	1950	
	1959	St. Lawrence Seaway opened; gave Ohio "ocean" ports
	1962	Feb 20 John Glenn of New Concord first American to orbit the earth
10,652,017	1970	

AREA: 41,222 sq. mi.

OKLAHOMA

46th

(Choctaw: "red people")

Osage, Kiowa, La Salle, Ft. Gibson, Cherokee, Creek, Chichasaw, Choctaw, Seminole, Okmulgee, Sequoyah, Guthrie, Glenn Pool, Will Rogers

The history of Oklahoma is largely the history of the American Indian—a story of broken promises, broken treaties. In the early 19th century, the western part of Louisiana Territory was considered Indian Territory, and President Jefferson believed that these remote lands would always provide space and freedom for the Indians. From Wisconsin, Illinois and Indiana, and from lands in Southeastern United States, members of a dozen tribes were brought to Indian Territory by the U.S. Government.

In Indian Territory, the "Five Civilized Tribes"—Cherokee, Creek, Choctaw, Chickasaw and Seminole—established independent nations under U.S. protection. These tribes developed farming, schools and courts; each had its capital where legislators assembled. Some of the farmers had slaves, and when the Civil War came, these tribes from the South sided with the Confederacy. After the war, the Federal Government felt justified in taking part of the Indian lands, and the process was repeated: lands were taken to build towns, roads, railroads. Indian Territory shrunk as parts were "opened" for white settlers. After formation of Oklahoma Territory (1890), there were actually twin territories—Indian and Oklahoma.

In spite of losses, the Indians quietly persisted and, in 1905, adopted a constitution and proposed to form a new State—Sequoyah. Rejected by Congress, they joined with Oklahoma Territory to achieve statehood. Over sixty tribes now live in Oklahoma.

Many white settlers farmed and raised cattle, but poor farming practices created the "Dust Bowl" in the west—an eroded wasteland that careful conservation has since reclaimed. Now wheat, cotton, hay and oats are profitable crops, and cattle ranches are found in every section.

The discovery of oil in 1889 brought a new source of wealth; Oklahoma ranks fourth in the production of oil and gas, first in helium, which is derived from gas. Many oil fields and refineries, and the headquarters of large oil companies, are located at Tulsa, the oil capital of the world.

POPULATION	DATE	HISTORIC EVENTS
	1682	LaSalle claimed land for France
	1803	Bought by U.S. in Louisiana Purchase
	1809	Indians of northwest (Delaware, Sac, Fox) moved to area
	1830	Congress established Indian Territory
	1831	Civilized tribes forcibly moved to area
	1844	Cherokees printed first Oklahoma newspaper, the *Advocate*
	1861	Civilized Tribes made treaties with Confederate States
	1866	Tribes alliance with Confederacy led U.S. to reclaim Indian lands
	1870	Indian leaders met at Okmulgee to form Confederation
	1889	Apr 22 First "run" of settlers into land previously held for Indians
258,657	1890	Became Oklahoma Territory; Guthrie capital
	1893	Dawes Commission liquidated Indian tribal governments
790,391	1900	
	1905	Indians adopted constitution; Congress refused them statehood Glenn Pool, first large oil field, discovered
	1907	Oklahoma & Indian Territories entered Union as 46th State
1,657,155	1910	Capital moved from Guthrie to Oklahoma City
	1916	Rich oil fields discovered in land of Osage Indians
2,396,040	1930	Farmers left the "Dust Bowl" in western section
2,336,434	1940	
2,559,253	1970	

AREA: 69,919 sq. mi.

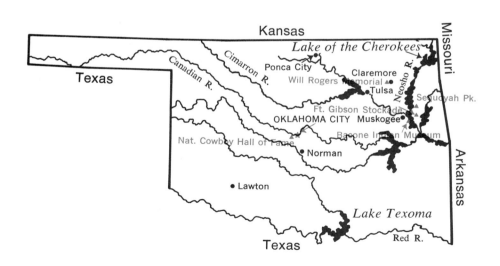

OREGON

(Algonquian: "beautiful water")

Chinook, Athabascan, Heceta, Gray,
Ft. Clatsop, Astoria, Columbia,
Ft. Vancouver, Oregon System

Oregon has more standing saw timber than any other State—and almost every year it leads the nation in lumbering. Ponderosa pine predominates in the Blue Mountains in the east, Douglas fir in the Coastal and Cascade ranges in the west. Between the western ranges, in the fertile Willamette valley, are many fruit farms as well as the State's principal cities—Portland, the largest; and Salem, the capital.

East of the Cascades, livestock graze on the open rangeland, and wheat, corn and barley are grown on the high plateau.

Before the white man came, over 100,000 Indians—the Athabascan, Chinook, Shoshone, and others—lived in Oregon country, which extended from the Pacific to the Continental Divide. In the nineteenth century these tribes were dispossessed and placed on reservations; some died fighting for their lands, some joined white communities. Today, approximately 8,000 Indians live in Oregon, half in reservations. Some entire villages bring their culture and traditions each year to the annual Pendleton Round-Up.

Thousands of pioneers endured the Oregon Trail over the mountains in covered wagons to settle in the valleys of the Willamette and Columbia Rivers.

One of Oregon's (and Washington's) most valuable resources, the Columbia River is—because of its exceptional flow and rapid fall—a tremendous source of water power, providing approximately one-third of the hydro-electric potential of the continental U.S. "Oregon" was the Indian name for this mighty river. It is navigable for ocean-going ships as far as Portland, the "City of Roses," which each June has its Rose Festival.

Since 1900 Oregon has contributed to popular government by the adoption of valuable political reforms—direct legislation through the initiative and referendum (1902), and popular selection of elected officials by primary election (1904), and procedures for recall of public officials. These reforms—the Oregon System—stand as the State's most distinctive, and most enduring, contribution to the American way of life.

POPULATION	DATE	HISTORIC EVENTS
	1775	Heceta claimed land for Spain
	1792	Capt. Gray discovered and named Columbia River
	1805	Lewis & Clark built Ft. Clatsop on Columbia
	1811	Astor's Pacific Fur Co. built Astoria at mouth of Columbia
	1818	British and U.S. agreed to joint occupation of Oregon
	1842	First immigration train arrived via Oregon Trail
	1846	U.S. and British agreed to present boundary
	1848	Became Oregon Territory
12,093	1850	Donation Land Act made land free to settlers
	1859	Joined Union as 33rd State
	1866	First cannery built on Columbia River
174,768	1880	
	1883	Transcontinental railroad reached Oregon
	1902	Oregon adopted initiative and referendum
	1904	Adopted primary election system
672,765	1910	
953,786	1930	Columbia River project begun
1,521,341	1950	
	1964	First off-shore oil and gas leases
2,091,385	1970	

AREA: 96,981 sq. mi.

81

PENNSYLVANIA 2nd

(Named by Charles II, after father of founder)

Delaware, Iroquois, Quaker,
Holy Experiment, Duquesne, Franklin,
Valley Forge, Independence Hall, Gettysburg

The middle one of the thirteen colonies, "The Keystone State" was also the cultural, economic, and, above all, political center of colonial America. William Penn was one of the first to build a society on the principles of civil and religious freedom, and his "Holy Experiment" provided rich soil for the growth of the ideas of freedom and liberty that flowered in Philadelphia in the *Declaration of Independence,* the *Articles of Confederation,* and finally, in the *Constitution of the United States.*

To a land sparsely settled by colonists from Sweden and Holland, William Penn brought Quakers from England and later attracted Germans, Welsh and Scotch-Irish. Penn treated the Delaware Indians fairly, and his colony prospered in peace. Not until the 1750s and the French and Indian War was there conflict with the Indians.

The scene of many Revolutionary War battles—and the desperate days at Valley Forge, this middle State also witnessed the Confederate Army's deepest penetration of the North: the mighty struggle at Gettysburg.

Like New York, Pennsylvania extends from an ocean port across the Appalachians to the Great Lakes. One of the great world ports, Philadelphia, with its rich heritage, remains today a cultural and industrial center and one of the nation's largest cities; it dominates eastern Pennsylvania as Pittsburgh does the west. America's steel capital, Pittsburgh leads in the production of iron and steel and such products as railroad cars and locomotives. In 1753, the twenty-one-year-old George Washington, while on a mission for the governor of Virginia, stood in the wilderness where the Monongahela and Allegheny rivers meet to form the Ohio, and noted it was "extremely well situated for a fort," and that site is today the "Golden Triangle" of Pittsburgh. This city built on hills lies in the heart of the richest coal fields in the U.S. To its north are oil fields that, over a century ago, began the petroleum era.

Besides William Penn, the State has had many famous citizens, but none more celebrated than that scientist, writer, philosopher and statesman, Benjamin Franklin.

POPULATION	DATE	HISTORIC EVENTS
	1643	Governor of New Sweden built fort at Upland (Chester)
	1655	Swedes relinquished control to Dutch
	1664	British seized control from Dutch
	1681	Charles II granted land to Penn, who sought refuge for Quakers
	1682	Principle of religious freedom established
	1683	Penn purchased land from Indians
	1751	Bell ordered from England to celebrate 50th anniversary of Charter of Privileges—became Liberty Bell
	1755	Gen. Braddock, with George Washington, defeated by French near Ft. Duquesne
	1760	British gained control of all Penn.
	1767	Charles Mason & Jeremiah Dixon surveyed Md.-Penn. border
	1774	First Continental Congress met in Philadelphia
	1775	Second Continental Congress met in Philadelphia
	1776	Congress adopted Declaration of Independence
	1777	Articles of Confederation drafted Washington and men at Valley Forge
	1787	Convention in Philadelphia drafted, adopted, U.S. Constitution
434,373	1790	Philadelphia became capital of U.S.
602,365	1800	U.S. capital moved from Philadelphia to Washington
	1859	First oil well in U.S. drilled at Titusville
2,906,215	1860	
	1863	Battle of Gettysburg
5,258,113	1890	
8,720,017	1920	
11,793,909	1970	

AREA: 45,333 sq. mi.

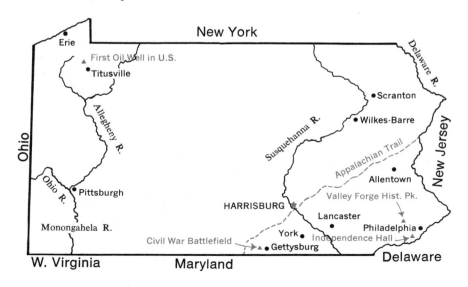

RHODE ISLAND

("red" island—for its red clay)

13th

Aquidneck, Verrazano, Roger Williams,
Greene, Stuart, Gladdings,
Slater, Newport

Rhode Island ranks fiftieth in size but it was one of the first of the thirteen colonies to declare independence from the British (two months before the Declaration of Independence), and independence has been a tradition there from its beginnings. In 1636 Roger Williams' independent spirit and belief in religious freedom drove him from Massachusetts to the wilderness to the south, where he founded Providence, the first free haven for religious worship in America. On the largest island in Narragansett Bay (Aquidneck or Rhode Island) other free-thinkers established Portsmouth and Newport, and these, together with Providence, were granted a royal charter as the Rhode Island and Providence Plantation—which is still the State's official name.

Prominent in colonial and revolutionary times were native sons General Nathaniel Greene, second in command to Washington, and Gilbert Stuart, foremost portrait artist of George Washington.

The first settlers farmed, fished and built ships which they used mainly to trade with other colonial ports: later, men like Samuel Slater developed the country's first textile mills, pioneering in America's industrial revolution. Since the eighteenth century, this 37-by-48 mile State has remained highly industrialized. Rhode Islanders still build ships (sailing and racing yachts), but they also manufacture textiles, electrical equipment, rubber and plastic goods, jewelry and silverware. Providence, the capital and New England's second largest city, is the costume jewelry center of the world.

Rhode Island's greatest natural resources are its coast and Narragansett Bay. On southern Aquidneck Island is one of the largest naval air stations and a major naval base, which includes the Naval War College. Here also is Newport, which since the 1720s has been a fashionable summer resort and, more recently, the site of music festivals and international yacht races and tennis tournaments. Other summer resorts are located on Block Island and on the western shore, from the bay to Watch Hill. With no other significant natural resources, our smallest State supports more people per square mile than any other.

POPULATION	DATE	HISTORIC EVENTS
	1564	Verrazano explored coastal area
	1636	Roger Williams founded Providence
	1638	First Baptist Congregation in U.S. established at Providence
	1644	Parliament established Providence Plantation
	1663	Charles II granted charter to Rhode Island and Providence Plantations
	1724	Franchise Law restricted vote to freeholders
	1763	Touro Synagogue founded on Aquidneck—first in U.S.
	1766	First dry goods store in America established—Gladdings of Providence
	1772	Providence citizens burned British ship *Gaspee*
	1776	May 4 General Assembly declared independence from British
		Dec 8 British Gen. Clinton seized Newport
68,825	1790	Samuel Slater built first cotton mill in America, at Pawtucket
	1814	First power loom in U.S. built at Peacedale
108,830	1840	
	1842	New constitution extended vote to non-freeholders
	1848	George Corliss of Providence developed steam engines for mills
276,531	1880	
	1885	First torpedo boat built at Bristol
604,397	1920	
949,723	1970	

AREA: 1,214 sq. mi.

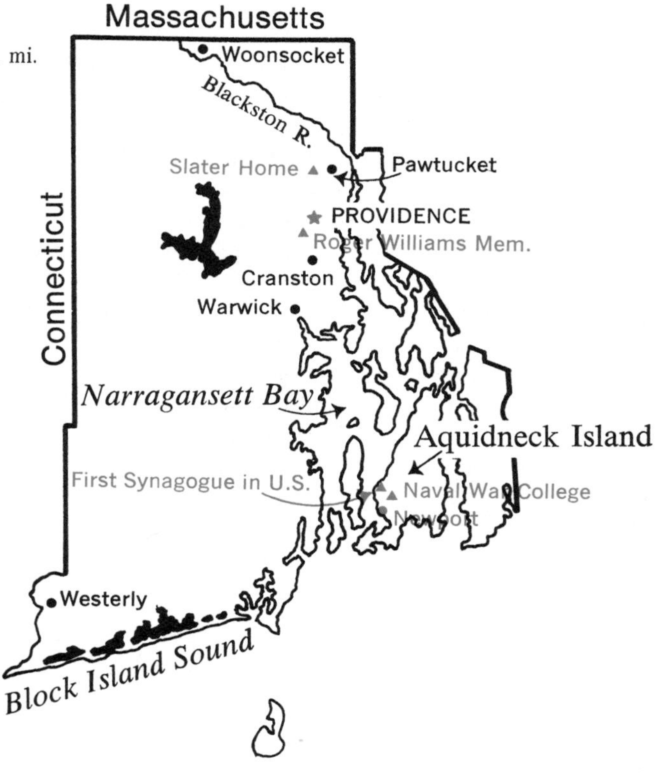

Massachusetts

Woonsocket

Blackston R.

Slater Home ▲ ● | Pawtucket

★ PROVIDENCE
▲ Roger Williams Mem.

● Cranston
Warwick ●

Connecticut

Narragansett Bay

Aquidneck Island

First Synagogue in U.S. | ▲ Naval War College
Newport

● Westerly

Block Island Sound

SOUTH CAROLINA

(After Charles II of England)

Catawba, Sewee, Cherokee, Vazquez,
Cooper, Middleton, Marion,
Calhoun, Ft. Sumter, Charleston

The first State to secede from the Union, South Carolina was also the scene of the first armed conflict of the Civil War—the Confederate attack on Fort Sumter. It suffered heavy losses when General Sherman marched through the State and burned the capital city, Columbia.

One of the principal plantation—and thus slave—States, South Carolina had for years led the struggle against the northern abolitionists and the Federal Government. In 1832 Senator—and former Vice President —John C. Calhoun of Abbeville, S.C., led the movement to nullify Federal tariffs against cotton, but secession was in the air even then. Until his death in 1850, Calhoun was the most prominent national figure defending the "State's rights" doctrine: that each State retained certain soverign powers and delegated only limited powers to the Federal Government when the Union was formed—a question that remains unsettled today in many areas of legislation.

In the Revolution, more battles (Ft. Moultrie, Cowpens, Charleston) were fought in South Carolina than in any other State. Native-son Francis Marion won fame leading State troops.

With coastal lowlands extending over 100 miles inland, South Carolina was well suited to the system of large plantations introduced in colonial days by Anthony Ashley Cooper. By 1800, cotton had become an important crop, and it remained the State's principal source of income through most of the nineteenth century. Eventually the lowlands turned also to tobacco, peanuts and soybeans, as well as cattle raising. In the up-country—to the north and west—industries developed: lumbering, furniture factories, textile mills (the State ranks second in textile production).

South Carolina has retained much of the flavor of the Old South, especially in and around Charleston, its first capital and most historic city. Here are well-preserved eighteenth- and nineteenth-century town houses, buildings and churches; nearby are plantation homes, as well as famous cypress and magnolia gardens. Middleton Place Gardens, carved out of the wilderness in 1741 by Henry Middleton, President of the First Continental Congress, are the oldest landscaped gardens in America.

POPULATION	DATE	HISTORIC EVENTS
	1526	Vazquez established first settlement
	1663	Charles II granted land to Earl of Clarendon
	1670	First permanent English settlement, at Albemarle Point
	1715	War with Sewee Indians
	1719	Became royal colony
	1729	South Carolina became separate colony
	1760	War with Cherokees
	1776	British fleet repulsed at Charleston
		Gen. Francis Marion defeated British
	1780	Gen. Clinton captured Charleston
	1781	Americans victorious at Cowpens
	1786	Capital established at Columbia
249,073	1790	
581,185	1830	
	1832	Ordinance of Nullification passed: forbid execution
		of Federal tariff in State
703,708	1860	First State to secede from Union
	1865	General Sherman marched across State, burned Columbia
	1868	Rejoined Union
1,340,316	1900	
1,899,804	1940	
2,590,516	1970	

AREA: 31,055 sq. mi.

SOUTH DAKOTA

40th

(Sioux: "allies")

Arikara, Sioux, Verendrye,
Crazy Horse, Red Cloud, Truteau,
Yankton, Homestake, Black Hills

The largest gold mine in the Western Hemisphere—the Homestake—is in the Black Hills of South Dakota. Discovered in 1876, this mine continues to produce millions of dollars worth of gold every year. Also in the Black Hills—a region revered by the Indians as the home of powerful spirits—is Mt. Rushmore, where the sculptor Gutzon Borglum carved the giant portraits in stone of Washington, Jefferson, Lincoln and Theodore Roosevelt.

The Missouri River cuts through the center of the State, separating the level prairie to the east from the western hills. In the east are large farms (averaging 1,000 acres) that produce wheat, corn, oats, barley and other field crops; in the west, huge cattle and sheep ranches. Today 92 per cent of the land is in farms and ranches.

South of the Black Hills are the fabled Badlands—grotesque eroded gorges and bare hills where scientists have discovered fossils of such prehistoric animals as humpless camels and horses with three toes.

For centuries, Dakota territory had been Indian country. In the seventeenth century the Arikara, or Ree, Indians held the land near the mouth of the Cheyenne River. Later came the Sioux, driven westward by the Chippewas, and Sioux tribes eventually claimed the entire area. As the frontier moved westward, the U.S. made a number of treaties with the Sioux; by 1868, the Sioux had given up all land east of the Missouri River for a "permanent" guarantee of all Dakota land west of the river.

General Custer's discovery of gold in the Black Hills in 1874—itself a violation of a treaty—led to further violations. The Sioux refused to rent or sell their sacred land, but the Government failed to protect it, and the violations increased. Under Chief Red Cloud, the Sioux retaliated and drove the Army out of its forts; Crazy Horse defeated Custer at the Little Big Horn. Later, Crazy Horse was slain, and the U.S. took possession of the Black Hills—and one of the world's most fabulous gold mines.

POPULATION	DATE	HISTORIC EVENTS
	1743	Verendrye explored South Dakota
	1780	Pierre Dorion settled near Yankton
	1794	Jean Truteau constructed first building, near Lake Andes
	1803	Became part of U.S. in Louisiana Purchase
	1804	Lewis & Clark explored area
	1823	Arikara Indians blocked Missouri R. to traders; defeated by U.S. troops
	1830	Sioux sold 12 million acres to U.S.
	1851	Sioux ceded further lands
	1859	Permanent settlement established at Yankton
	1861	Became Dakota Territory; Yankton capital
	1868	Great Sioux Reservation formed: all land west of Missouri R.
11,776	1870	
	1874	Gen. Custer discovered gold in Black Hills (Sioux land)
	1876	Sioux War: Crazy Horse defeated Custer
		Gold discovered in Homestake area
98,268	1880	
	1881	Northern Pacific R.R. completed line through Dakota Terr.
	1889	Joined Union (with N. Dakota) as twin States
348,600	1890	U.S. troops massacred Chief Big Foot and over 200 Indians at Wounded Knee Creek
583,888	1910	
666,257	1970	

AREA: 77,047 sq. mi.

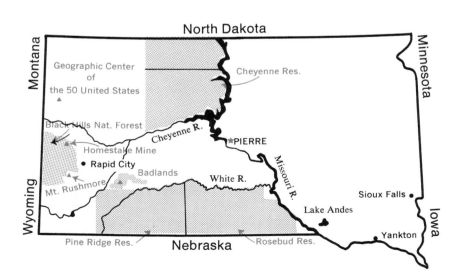

(Name of Cherokee village)

Cherokee, Chickasaw, Creek, Shawnee,
Boone, Crockett, Jackson, Polk,
Shiloh, Johnson, Handy, Oak Ridge

Originally part of the Carolina colony, Tennessee had to struggle more than most to become a State. As early as 1772, Watauga settlers attempted to establish a community independent of the British Royal Colony, and in 1784, the pioneers living between the mountains and the Mississippi River formed the State of Franklin and applied to the Continental Congress for recognition. With its own governor and legislature, Franklin existed until 1788, when it rejoined North Carolina—to be ceded to the U.S. Government as Federal Territory. Once the Territory reached the required 60,000 population, it was able to become a State.

Tennessee divides naturally into three regions. In the east the broad valley of the Tennessee River lies between the Blue Ridge and Cumberland Mountains. To this region, the Tennessee Valley Authority has, with three large dams, brought flood control and low-cost power, which supports growing textile and chemical industries. Here also are the nation's richest sources of zinc and marble, and, at Oak Ridge, the plant that made the first atomic bomb.

In the central section, the bluegrass basin of rolling hills and valleys has farms that raise corn, hay and tobacco, cattle and dairy products.

Western Tennessee—from the western part of the Tennessee River to the Mississippi River—has level, fertile land that is largely devoted to cotton. Here also is Memphis, a river port and the State's largest city. Each May it is the scene of the traditional Cotton Festival.

During the Civil War over 800 battles and skirmishes were fought in Tennessee—more than in any other State except Virginia. National military parks commemorate such battles as Shiloh, Stone's River, Chickamauga and Chattanooga.

National historical landmarks in the State include The X-Ten reactor at Oak Ridge; Memphis's Beale St.—home of W. C. Handy, father of the blues; and The Hermitage, east of Nashville—the home of President Andrew Jackson.

POPULATION	DATE	HISTORIC EVENTS
	1663	Area was part of Carolina grant of Charles II
	1768	William Bean established first permanent settlement, on Watauga River
	1772	Watauga settlers declared independence from British
	1775	Part of area purchased from Cherokees
	1777	Became Washington County of N. Carolina
	1784	Settlers applied to Congress for recognition as new State of Franklin
	1789	Carolina ceded Tennessee lands to U.S. Govt., under provisions of Northwest Ordinance
35,691	1790	
	1796	Joined Union as 16th State
	1828	Andrew Jackson elected 7th U.S. President
681,904	1830	
	1844	James Polk elected 11th U.S. President
1,109,801	1860	
	1861	Seceded from Union (E. Tenn. voted to remain in Union)
	1862	Gen. Grant won battle of Shiloh
	1863	Confederates won at Chickamauga, Union at Chattanooga
	1865	Andrew Johnson became 17th U.S. President
		Ku Klux Klan organized at Pulaski
	1866	First Confederate State to rejoin Union
2,020,616	1900	
	1933	TVA established
2,915,841	1940	
3,924,164	1970	

AREA: 41,687 sq. mi.

TEXAS

(Indian: "friend")

28th

*Karankawan, De Soto, El Paso,
Houston, Bowie, Crockett,
Spindletop, Space Flight Center*

Texas is big. No longer the largest State, it yet dwarfs any of the other forty-seven contiguous States. Big in size, it is also big in its history, products, and people.

Once an independent republic (1836-45), Texas is the only State that entered the Union with the right to divide itself into more States—a right that Texas has always been too big to exercise.

With violence and heroism that have become legend, Texas was wrested from the infant Mexican nation by Americans from nearby territories. Those Texas heroes—Sam Houston, Jim Bowie, and Davy Crockett —fought for freedom and for the land, but they could never have imagined the vast wealth hidden beneath the surface. In 1543, DeSoto's men found patches of oil floating on the coastal waters, but the riches slumbering beneath Texas soil were not known to the world until 1901, when the Spindletop gusher, near Beaumont, blew in—producing a record 100,000 barrels a day. Today almost half of the oil and natural gas produced in the U.S. comes from Texas. The State is also the greatest U.S. source of salt, magnesium and sulphur, and one of the largest producers of helium.

The largest city is Houston, with its oil refineries, mills, and chemical plants, and the famous covered stadium, the Astrodome. Dallas is in the heart of the oil and cotton region; Ft. Worth is the cattle capital.

With more farms than any other State, Texas is a leading producer of both livestock—cattle, sheep, goats—and crops—cotton, rice, sorghum. Six million acres are irrigated. The celebrated King ranch is larger than the State of Rhode Island.

In several ways Texas is a border State: not only does it provide the U.S. border for 800 miles along the Rio Grande, but, within its boundaries, four distinct cultures meet—the woodlands, the plains, the desert, and the seacoast. And, with the establishment of the Manned Spacecraft Center at Houston, there is a fifth. The long-horn steer, the oil well, and now outer space—that is Texas.

POPULATION	DATE	HISTORIC EVENTS
	1528	Cabeza de Vaca visited Karankawan tribes
	1541	Coronado explored area
	1543	DeSoto explored coast
	1682	Spanish established first settlement, near El Paso
	1691	Area became a Spanish province
	1821	Became part of Mexico
	1835	U.S. settlers revolted against Mexican rule
	1836	March 6 Mexicans killed 187 Texans at the Alamo
		April 6 Sam Houston defeated Mexicans at San Jacinto; Republic of Texas formed
	1839	Texas troops drove Cherokees into Mexico
	1845	Joined Union as 28th State
212,592	1850	
	1861	Seceded from Union
	1865	Slaves freed
	1866	First oil well drilled in Texas
818,579	1870	Rejoined the Union
3,048,710	1900	
	1901	Spindletop gusher, near Beaumont, largest well discovered
5,824,715	1930	
9,579,677	1960	
	1963	Manned Space Flight Center built at Houston
11,196,730	1970	

AREA: 267,339 sq. mi.

UTAH

(Navajo: "upper")

Shoshone, Ute, Escalante & Dominguez,
Ogden, Robidoux, Deseret, Brigham
Young, Provo, Tabernacle Choir

"This is the place!" Brigham Young said when he led the first Mormon settlers into Salt Lake Valley in 1847, a year before the U.S. acquired the territory from Mexico. There, after a thousand-mile trek to escape persecution, members of the Mormon Church established the first permanent white settlement in Utah. At that time, the area was sparsely populated with Paiutes, Shoshones and Navajos.

Pioneering in irrigation, the well-organized Mormons brought water from the Wasatch Mountains to cultivate the rich, arid valley and soon built thriving farms—with the help of seagulls that, in 1848, miraculously appeared to destroy swarms of crickets and save the crops. The valley settlement became the center of the Mormon's expanding community, and modern Salt Lake City, with its Tabernacle and shrines, remains the center of the State and of Mormon culture today.

Like neighboring states, Utah has large, practically unpopulated areas dominated by extremes of climate—mountains in the northeast, the Great Salt Lake Desert in the west, and vast plateaus and striking gorges and geological formations in the south.

Utah Territory had a tumultuous and prolonged history. From the time the Territory was established, the Mormon practice of polygamy caused friction with the Federal Government; in 1857 it led to the Utah War, in which the U.S. Army did little more than occupy the area. The Army's discovery of valuable ore deposits and the completion of the railroad brought others to the Territory, but the Mormons' struggle with the Federal Government continued; Congress passed anti-polygamy laws and imprisoned thousands. Finally, in 1890, the Church renounced polygamy; and in 1896 the way was open for Utah to join the Union—after forty-six years as a Territory.

Still dominated by Mormon culture, modern Utah has developed manufacturing to more than match its extensive farming—raising cattle, poultry and field crops. Mining (copper, oil, iron, coal and uranium), copper and petroleum refining, building guided missiles, and steel making are principal industries. Near Provo is the largest steel plant in the West.

Best known of Mormon achievements is the Mormon Tabernacle in Salt Lake City—and its distinguished Tabernacle Choir.

POPULATION	DATE	HISTORIC EVENTS
	1776	Spanish missionaries Escalante and Dominguez explored area
	1824	Trappers Bridger and Ogden discovered Great Salt Lake
	1837	Antoine Robidoux established first post
	1843	Fremont led first U.S. Expedition in area
	1847	Mormons established first permanent settlement
	1848	Seagulls saved crops
	1849	Mormons established State of Deseret
		Became Utah Territory
11,380	1850	Bingham discovered ore deposits
	1852	First iron mining near Cedar City
	1857	Utah War—U.S. Army occupied Utah
	1858	First lead mining and smelting, in Beaver County
	1865	Ute-Black Hawk War; last major Indian struggle in area
	1869	Transcontinental railroads completed through Utah
86,786	1870	
	1882	Congress passed anti-polygamy law
210,779	1890	Mormon Church suspended practice of polygamy
	1896	Joined Union as 45th State
507,847	1930	
1,059,273	1970	

AREA: 84,916 sq. mi.

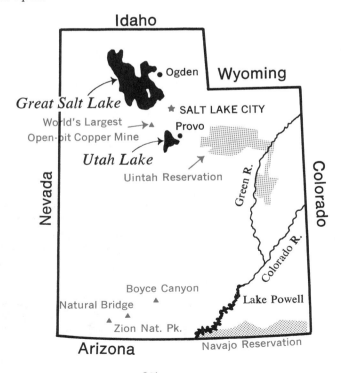

95

VERMONT

(French: "green mountain")

14th

*Algonquian, Iroquois, Champlain,
Fort Dummer, Ethan Allen,
Bennington, Arthur, Coolidge, Stowe*

The only inland New England State, Vermont lies between Lake Champlain and the Connecticut River, its Green Mountains extending from Massachusetts to Canada. For years this wilderness was claimed by both New Hampshire and New York, a dispute settled only when Ethan and Ira Allen and the Green Mountain Boys drove the New Yorkers out of what was then called the "New Hampshire Grants" and helped establish an independent republic. The constitution adopted in 1777 was the first in America to provide for a State system of education, to give every man the right to vote, and to forbid slavery. A sovereign state for fourteen years, Vermont fought in the Revolution along with the thirteen colonies—and it was the first State to join the newly formed United States.

As in other New England States, Vermont had the township as the basic unit of government, and the Vermont Town Meeting has for centuries been a striking example of democracy in action.

The rocky, forested mountains that dominate Vermont have, in innumerable ways, shaped its history. Early settlers found the thin soil on the sloping land was best for raising sheep and dairy cattle; below the surface, others found a wealth of granite and marble. Vermont still has many dairy farms—and a number that produce its famous maple syrup. Vermont marble is part of such well known structures as the United Nations Building. Near Barre is the largest granite quarry in the world.

Vermont forests (over 70 per cent of the State) support large lumber and paper industries, and near its few, comparatively small cities are plants producing tools, machinery and textiles.

The mountains, lakes and forests of Vermont, coupled with the relatively dry climate, have long attracted vacationers, hunters, and campers to enjoy the cool summers and, in the autumn, the spectacular foliage. Since 1934, when the first ski tow in the United States was built at Woodstock, Vermont has also been one of the most popular winter resort areas. Stowe, near Mt. Mansfield, is considered one of the East's leading ski resorts.

THE GREEN MOUNTAIN STATE

POPULATION	DATE	HISTORIC EVENTS
	1609	Samuel Champlain crossed Lake Champlain
	1666	First white settlement, Ft. St. Anne, built on Isle La Motte
	1724	First permanent English settlement, Ft. Dummer on Connecticut R.
	1750	Vermont lands granted to N.H. royal governor Wentworth
	1764	Royal order gave disputed lands to N.Y.
	1770	Committees of safety formed in Vermont towns
	1775	May 10 Green Mountain Boys captured Ft. Ticonderoga
	1776	Convention held to consider statehood
	1777	Jan 16 Independent republic of New Connecticut formed
		Aug 16 Gen. Stark defeated Gen. Burgoyne at Old Bennington
	1779	Legislature planned 6-mile-square towns
	1784	First marble quarry in U.S. near Manchester
85,425	1790	
	1791	Joined Union as 14th State
	1805	Montpelier chosen capital
217,895	1810	
291,948	1840	
	1881	Chester Arthur of Fairfield became 21st U.S. President
352,428	1920	
	1923	Calvin Coolidge of Plymouth Notch became 30th U.S. President
444,732	1970	

AREA: 9,609 sq. mi.

(After Elizabeth I, Virgin Queen of England)

Jamestown, Williamsburg, Henry, Washington, Yorktown, Jefferson, Madison, Monroe, Harrison, Tyler, Taylor, Lee, Appomattox, Wilson

The first colony established in America, Virginia has been called "The Mother of Presidents" and "The Cavalier State"—and the democratic and aristocratic strains suggested by these titles are woven deeply into Virginia's history: one can be traced to Jamestown, to the first representative assembly in the world, and to Patrick Henry and Thomas Jefferson; the other to the first use of slaves in America, to royal grants of vast areas of land, to the plantation system, and to the royal cavaliers who fled to Virginia during the English Civil War.

Largest and wealthiest of the colonies, Virginia had the power and the central location to assume a position of leadership—and, in time of crisis, she produced the gifted leaders who contributed so much in shaping the new nation and in directing it through its first thirty years. How remarkable that four of the nation's first five Presidents came from Virginia—Washington, Jefferson, Madison and Monroe!

Although Virginia lost its vast western lands—part of the Northwest Territory and the lands that became Kentucky and West Virginia, it retained enough territory to remain, throughout our history, a dominant State with an extensive coast and considerable shipping and ship-building; with fertile lowlands punctuated by navigable rivers—where tobacco has been raised since colonial days; and with two ranges of forested mountains. And this land has served as the theater for many dramatic moments in American history—from Washington's victory at Yorktown to the terrible Civil War battles at Manassas and Chancellorsville and the quiet surrender at Appomattox. In northern Virginia, on the southern shore of the Potomac overlooking the nation's capital, are such modern monuments as Arlington National Cemetery, the massive Pentagon, the Iwo Jima Memorial and the Tomb of the Unknown Soldier. Further South, overlooking the Potomac, is Washington's estate at Mount Vernon, and, near the center of the State, outside Charlottesville, is Monticello, the magnificent creation of Jefferson's that almost rivals his greatest creation, which is perhaps the greatest of *any* Virginian's—*The Declaration of Independence.*

POPULATION	DATE	HISTORIC EVENTS
	1607	First permanent English settlement in America established at Jamestown
	1619	First Negro slaves introduced
		First meeting of House of Burgesses, first representative assembly
	1699	Williamsburg made the capital
	1766	Patrick Henry attacked Stamp Act
	1775	March 20 Henry delivered famous speech before Convention in Richmond
		June 14 Continental Congress elected Washington Commander-in-Chief
	1776	George Mason's Bill of Rights adopted for State
		July 4 Jefferson's *Declaration of Independence* approved by Congress
	1781	Cornwallis surrendered at Yorktown
	1784	Virginia ceded part of its western lands to Federal government
	1788	Tenth State to ratify Constitution
	1789	Washington elected 1st U.S. President
807,557	1800	Jefferson elected 3rd U.S. President
	1801	John Marshall became Justice of Supreme Court
1,025,227	1840	William Harrison elected 9th U.S. President
	1861	Seceded from Union; Richmond made Confederate capital
		Robert E. Lee made Commander of Confederate forces
	1865	Lee surrendered at Appomattox
1,225,163	1870	Rejoined the Union
2,061,612	1910	
	1941-5	Gen. George Marshall led U.S. Army during World War II
3,318,680	1950	
4,648,494	1970	

AREA: 40,815 sq. mi.

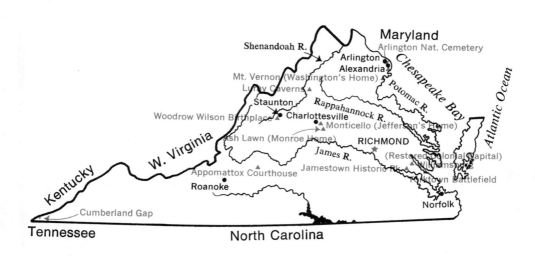

99

WASHINGTON

42nd

(After George Washington)

Yakima, Nez Perce, Cayuse, Walla Walla,
Columbia, Vancouver, Cascades,
Mt. Rainier, Grand Coulee, Hanford

Rich in the prime resources of water power and timber, and blessed with well-protected harbors in Puget Sound, Washington also enjoys a location that has made her the gateway to Alaska and the Orient. Her largest city— Seattle—is the leading port and the commercial and cultural center of the Northwest. Her Space Needle, with a revolving restaurant 607 feet above the Seattle Center, is part of the permanent complex built for the Seattle World's Fair.

The Switzerland of America, Washington has rugged Alpine scenery in both the Olympic Mountains on the peninsula and the Cascade Range, which extends through the middle of the State from Canada to Oregon, with Mt. Rainier its highest peak (14,410). Competing with these wonders are the Columbia, the largest river flowing into the Pacific and the greatest power stream in the civilized world, and Grand Coulee, a multi-purpose conservation project and the world's largest concrete dam. Bonneville, Dalles, Grand Coulee, and other dams provide power for a growing number of industries, and irrigation for farms raising apples, berries and other fruits.

In the nineteenth century, pioneers and woodsmen freely cut the fir, pine, hemlock and other evergreens that covered the mountains, and for a time Washington ranked first in producing timber, but at great cost. Conservation practices instituted after 1900 helped preserve the forests, and today over half the State remains forest land. In eastern Washington most of the open grazing ranges disappeared when the railroad was completed in the 1880s, and farming, industry and trade increased.

The most densely populated State in the Northwest, Washington has, in the Air Age, become a center for processing aluminum and manufacturing airplanes. Significant also are its fisheries and chemical and food-processing plants. And it is the home of the great Hanford works of the Atomic Energy Commission.

100

POPULATION	DATE	HISTORIC EVENTS
	1592	Juan de Fuca discovered inlet to Puget Sound
	1774	Juan Perez of Spain sighted Mt. Olympus
	1778	Cap. John Cook of England sailed coast
	1792	George Vancouver of England explored Puget Sound
		Robert Gray of Boston discovered and named Columbia R.— gave U.S. first claim to area
	1805	Lewis and Clark crossed area, east to west
	1810	David Thompson of Northwest Co. built first permanent structure, on Spokane R.
	1818	British and U.S. agreed on joint occupation of area for ten years
	1824	John McLoughlin of Hudson Bay Co became "governor"
	1845	First permanent U.S. settlement at Tumwater
	1847	Smithfield (Later Olympia) established near Tumwater
1,201	1850	Port Townsend settled
	1851	Seattle founded
	1853	Became Washington Territory
	1872	Spokane founded
75,116	1880	
	1883	Northern Pacific R.R. completed to coast
	1889	Joined Union as 42nd State
1,141,990	1910	
2,378,963	1950	
	1962	World's Fair at Seattle
3,409,169	1970	

AREA: 68,192 sq. mi.

101

WEST VIRGINIA

35th

*Iroquois, Cherokee, Shawnee, Delaware,
Kanawha, Morgan ap Morgan, Harper's
Ferry, White Sulphur Springs*

West Virginia was born in the Civil War: it seceded from Virginia when that State seceded from the Union, but for almost a century differences as significant as the bordering mountains had separated eastern and western Virginia—disputes over the apportionment of taxes, representation, and funds for public works. There were also fundamental social and economic differences: in the 1800s eastern Virginia was essentially an agricultural and aristocratic society, based on slavery; settlers in the west, most of whom were against slavery, were producing salt, coal and lumber, and building and operating the area's first textile mills. The unusual shape of the State, with its northern and eastern panhandles, resulted from the settlement of earlier border disputes with Pennsylvania and Maryland and, later, from the Virginia counties that chose to form the new State.

West Virginia grew rapidly as an industrial State after 1870, when the railroad linked it with coastal cities. Some of its resources—coal, oil and timber—were shipped extensively, but these, along with such others as salt brine, water, clay and sand, permitted the development of local steel, chemical, ceramic and glassware industries.

Natural resources have continued to play an important role in the State's growth. For a quarter century West Virginia has led the nation in mining bituminous coal and producing metallurgical coke. It ranks second in the production of natural gas. And its forests of beech, maple, oak and hickory make hardwood lumber an important product.

West Virginia has more mountains than any other State east of the Rockies. Its forests and many rivers and lakes offer both summer and winter recreation. National forests provide almost one million acres for hunting and fishing. The State has over 200 significant natural springs—the largest, Big Spring, near Masonville; the most famous, Berkeley Springs and White Sulphur Springs, celebrated resorts as old as the nation.

102

POPULATION	DATE	HISTORIC EVENTS
	1671	Abraham Wood of England explored area
	1716	Governor Spotswood of Virginia vistied area
	1719	First settlers came from Md. and Penn.
	1726	Morgan ap Morgan established first permanent settlement at Millcreek
	1742	John Salley discovered bituminous coal near Racine
	1747	Washington surveyed lands in area
	1749	Jacob Marlin and Stephen Sewell established first settlement west of Alleghenies
	1782	Final battle of Revolution: American victory at Ft. Henry
55,873	1790	
	1794	Gen. "Mad Anthony" Wayne won decisive battle over Indians
	1829	Constitutional convention held to separate from Va.
	1859	John Brown seized arsenal at Harper's Ferry
376,688	1860	
	1861	June 3 First land battle of Civil War at Philippi Apr 17 W. Va. legislators voted against secession
	1863	Joined Union as 35th State
618,457	1880	
	1885	Capital moved from Wheeling to Charleston
1,463,701	1920	
2,005,552	1950	
1,744,237	1970	

AREA: 24,181 sq. mi.

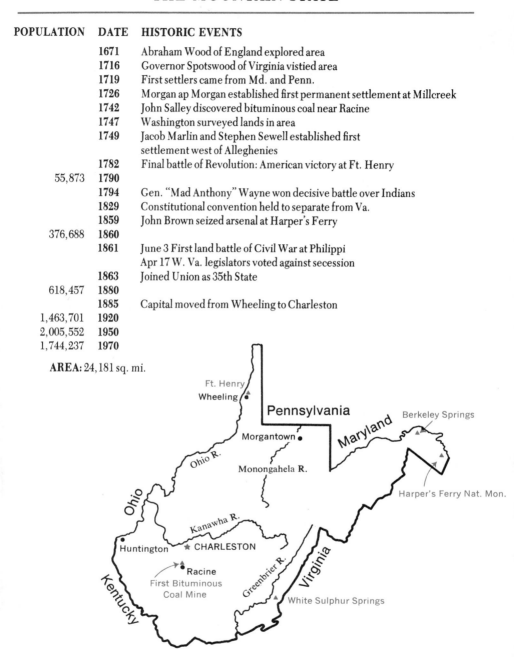

WISCONSIN

30th

(Chippewa: "gathering of the waters")

*Winnebago, Fox, Nicolet, Allouez, Marquette,
Joliet, Ripon, Ringling Brothers,
La Follette, Frank Lloyd Wright*

The dairy capital of America, Wisconsin also leads the nation in the production of beer.

The State's 8500 lakes and 10,000 rivers and streams were enjoyed exclusively by Indians and a few trappers until Welsh and English settlers came from the South in the 1820s and 1830s to work the lead mines and stone quarries in the southeast section. Later, immigrants came from Germany, Poland, Holland and the Scandinavian countries to start the dairy, poultry and hog farms found throughout the State. Many newcomers worked at lumbering, and, for a time, Wisconsin produced more timber than any other State; today it produces paper and woodpulp.

One of the first States to join the Granger movement—a fraternal and political organization, Wisconsin also pioneered important progressive social legislation, such as the income-tax and primary-election laws.

A towering figure in Wisconsin's history was Robert La Follette. Elected governor in 1901, he championed reform programs that freed the State from the control of big business and made possible honest, effective government.

Although still a leading farm State, twentieth-century Wisconsin has considerable industry and trade—most concentrated in cities near Lake Michigan. There factories make tractors, auto engines and parts, hardware, and furniture, as well as most of the beer produced in the State. Milwaukee, the largest city, is a growing industrial and cultural center and, with the opening of the St. Lawrence Seaway, an international port.

Wisconsin's famous sons include writer Hamlin Garland, military flying pioneer General Billy Mitchell, historian Frederick Jackson Turner, and architect Frank Lloyd Wright.

POPULATION	DATE	HISTORIC EVENTS
	1634	French explorer Nicolet made treaty with Winnebagos
	1665	Fr. Claude Allouez established first permanent mission on Chequamegon Bay
	1673	Marquette and Joliet went down Fox and Wisconsin Rivers to discover Mississippi R.
	1689	Perrot claimed area for France
	1763	France ceded Wisconsin lands to Britain
	1783	Became part of U.S.; British Northwest Co. retained control
	1787	Became part of Northwest Territory
	1816	U.S. forces drove out last of British
	1824	First lead mining in southwest Wisconsin
	1829	U.S. gained land through treaties with Indians
	1836	Became Wisconsin Territory
30,945	1840	
	1846	Joined Union as 30th State
305,391	1850	
	1854	First steps to organize Republican Party, at Ripon
	1856	Margarethe Schurz opened first kindergarten in America in Watertown
775,881	1860	
	1884	Ringling Bros. first circus organized at Baraboo
1,693,330	1890	
	1901	Robert La Follette elected reform governor
2,632,067	1920	
3,434,575	1950	
4,417,933	1970	

AREA: 56,154 sq. mi.

(Delaware: "end of the plains")

Shoshone, Sioux, Arapahoe, Kiowa,
Bannock, Grand Teton, Yellowstone,
Fitzpatrick, Ft. Laramie, Esther Morris

Wyoming is the only State made up of land from all four principal annexations to the original United States—the Louisiana Purchase, and the Texas, Mexican and Oregon Cessions. The Continental Divide follows a series of ranges through Wyoming, from the northwest to the center of the State's southern boundary, separating the headwaters of the West's mightiest rivers—the Colorado, Missouri, and Columbia.

The second highest State (average elevation: 6700 Ft.), Wyoming has a variety of natural wonders: Devil's Tower, a geologic mass that thrusts itself from the plain's floor; the Grand Tetons, perhaps the world's most dramatic mountains; and Yellowstone, with its springs, volcanoes and famous geysers—the nation's oldest and largest national park. For generations, thousands of Arapahoe, Sioux, Shoshone, Bannock, Kiowa, and Pawnee lived in Wyoming. The warring tribes—especially the Arapahoe—controlled eastern Wyoming; the friendly Shoshone lived in the west. Today approximately 4000 members of both tribes live together at Wind River Reservation, a 1.8-million-acre tract whose oil and natural gas deposits bring royalties of almost $2 million a year. Buried on the reservation is Sacajawea, the Shoshone girl guide of the Lewis and Clark expedition.

Until 1840, the Indians—and a few trappers—had the plains and high plateaus of Wyoming to themselves. Shortly after, a stream of immigrants crossed Wyoming on the Oregon, Mormon and California Trails, and the first settlers arrived. Pioneers discovered that the range grass provided excellent grazing for cattle and sheep, and Texas cattlemen brought huge herds, at times overstocking the ranges. Cattle raising remains a key industry, surpassed only by oil refining. Besides ample oil and natural gas, Wyoming has one of the largest coal reserves in the nation.

Of particular importance has been the State's role in establishing equal rights for women. Under the leadership of Esther Hobart Morris, Wyoming Territory became the first government in the world to grant women equal rights.

POPULATION	DATE	HISTORIC EVENTS
	1807	John Colter of Lewis & Clark Expedition, explored area
	1824	Thos. Fitzpatrick led group across Continental Divide
	1834	Ft. Laramie built
	1842	Fitzpatrick led first wagon train over Oregon Trail through Wyoming
	1861	First telegraph line to Pacific connected in Wyoming
	1866	Sioux killed Col. Fetterman and 81 men near Ft. Kearny
	1867	Gold discovered at S. Pass
	1868	Peace with Sioux Chief Red Cloud
		Became Wyoming Territory
	1869	Legislature gave women right to vote
9,118	1870	Esther Hobart Morris, "Mother of Women Suffrage," first woman appointed Justice of Peace
	1872	Yellowstone Nat. Pk. established—first Nat. Pk.
	1883	First oil well drilled, near Lander
62,555	1890	Joined Union as 44th State
	1906	Devil's Tower proclaimed first National Monument
145,965	1910	First woman elected to Wyoming Legislature
	1912	Oil boom near Casper
	1925	Mrs. Nellie Tayloe Ross became first woman governor in U.S.
250,742	1940	
332,416	1970	

AREA: 97,914 sq. mi.

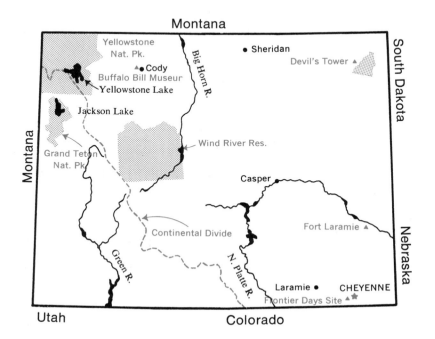

STATE	ENTERED UNION		CAPITAL	AREA		POPULATION	
	Date	No.		Sq. Mi.	Rank	1970	Rank
Alabama	1819	22	Montgomery	51,609	29	3,444,165	21
Alaska	1959	49	Juneau	586,400	1	302,173	50
Arizona	1912	48	Phoenix	113,909	6	1,772,482	33
Arkansas	1836	25	Little Rock	53,104	27	1,923,295	32
California	1850	31	Sacramento	158,693	3	19,953,134	1
Colorado	1876	38	Denver	104,247	8	2,207,259	30
Connecticut	1788	5	Hartford	5,009	48	3,032,217	24
Delaware	1787	1	Dover	2,057	49	548,104	46
Florida	1845	27	Tallahassee	58,560	22	6,789,443	9
Georgia	1788	4	Atlanta	58,876	21	4,589,575	15
Hawaii	1959	50	Honolulu	6,424	47	769,913	40
Idaho	1890	43	Boise	83,557	13	713,008	42
Illinois	1818	21	Springfield	56,400	24	11,113,976	5
Indiana	1816	19	Indianapolis	36,291	38	5,193,669	11
Iowa	1846	29	Des Moines	56,290	25	2,825,041	25
Kansas	1861	34	Topeka	82,264	14	2,249,071	28
Kentucky	1792	15	Frankfort	40,395	37	3,219,311	22
Louisiana	1812	18	Baton Rouge	48,523	31	3,643,180	20
Maine	1820	23	Augusta	33,215	39	993,663	38
Maryland	1788	7	Annapolis	10,577	42	3,922,399	18
Massachusetts	1788	6	Boston	8,257	45	5,689,170	10
Michigan	1837	26	Lansing	58,216	23	8,875,083	7
Minnesota	1858	32	St. Paul	84,068	12	3,805,069	19
Mississippi	1817	20	Jackson	47,716	32	2,216,912	29
Missouri	1821	24	Jefferson City	69,686	19	4,677,399	13

FLOWER	BIRD	TREE
Camellia	Yellowhammer	Southern Pine
Forget-me-not	Willow Ptarmigan	Sitka Spruce
Saguaro	Cactus Wren	Paloverde
Apple Blossom	Mockingbird	Pine
California Poppy	Valley Quail	Redwood
Columbine	Lark Bunting	Colorado Blue Spruce
Mountain Laurel	American Robin	White Oak
Peach Blossom	Blue Hen Chicken	American Holly
Orange Blossom	Mockingbird	Sabal Palm
Cherokee Rose	Brown Thrasher	Live Oak
Hibiscus	Hawaiian Goose	Kukui
Lewis Mock Orange	Mountain Bluebird	Western White Pine
Native Violet	Cardinal	Bur Oak
Peony	Cardinal	Tulip
Wild Rose	Eastern Goldfinch	Oak
Sunflower	Western Meadow Lark	Cottonwood
Golden Rod	Cardinal	Tuliptree
Southern Magnolia	Eastern Brown Pelican	Bald Cypress
Pine Cone	Chickadee	Eastern White Pine
Black-eyed Susan	Baltimore Oriole	White Oak
Mayflower	Chickadee	American Elm
Apple Blossom	Robin	White Pine
Showy Lady's-slipper	Loon	Red Pine
Magnolia	Mockingbird	Magnolia
Hawthorn	Eastern Bluebird	Dogwood

STATE	ENTERED UNION		CAPITAL	AREA		POPULATION	
	Date	*No.*		*Sq. Mi.*	*Rank*	*1970*	*Rank*
Montana	1889	41	Helena	147,138	4	694,409	43
Nebraska	1867	37	Lincoln	77,227	15	1,483,791	35
Nevada	1864	36	Carson City	110,540	7	488,738	47
New Hampshire	1788	9	Concord	9,304	44	737,681	41
New Jersey	1787	3	Trenton	8,219	46	7,168,164	8
New Mexico	1912	47	Sante Fe	121,666	5	1,016,000	37
New York	1788	11	Albany	49,576	30	18,190,740	2
North Carolina	1789	12	Raleigh	52,712	28	5,082,059	12
North Dakota	1889	39	Bismarck	70,665	17	617,761	45
Ohio	1803	17	Columbus	41,222	35	10,652,017	6
Oklahoma	1907	46	Oklahoma City	69,919	18	2,559,253	27
Oregon	1859	33	Salem	96,981	10	2,091,385	31
Pennsylvania	1787	2	Harrisburg	45,333	33	11,793,909	3
Rhode Island	1790	13	Providence	1,214	50	949,723	39
South Carolina	1788	8	Columbia	31,055	40	2,590,516	26
South Dakota	1889	40	Pierre	77,047	16	666,257	44
Tennessee	1796	16	Nashville	42,244	34	3,924,164	17
Texas	1845	28	Austin	267,339	2	11,196,730	4
Utah	1896	45	Salt Lake City	84,916	11	1,059,273	36
Vermont	1791	14	Montpelier	9,609	43	444,732	48
Virginia	1788	10	Richmond	40,815	36	4,648,494	14
Washington	1889	42	Olympia	68,192	20	3,409,169	22
West Virginia	1863	35	Charleston	24,181	41	1,744,237	34
Wisconsin	1848	30	Madison	56,154	26	4,417,933	16
Wyoming	1890	44	Cheyenne	97,914	9	332,416	49

FLOWER	BIRD	TREE
Bitterroot	Western Meadow Lark	Ponderosa Pine
Goldenrod	Western Meadow Lark	American Elm
Sagebrush	Mountain Bluebird	Single-leaf Pinon
Common Lilac	Purple Finch	White Birch
Purple Violet	Eastern Goldfinch	Red Oak
Yucca	Road Runner	Pinon
Rose	Bluebird	Sugar Maple
Dogwood	Cardinal	Pine
Wild Prairie Rose	Western Meadow Lark	American Elm
Scarlet Carnation	Cardinal	Ohio Buckeye
Mistletoe	Scissor-tailed Flycatcher	Redbud
Oregon Grape	Western Meadow Lark	Douglas Fir
Mountain Laurel	Ruffed Grouse	Eastern Hemlock
Violet	Rhode Island Red	Red Maple
Yellow Jessamine	Carolina Wren	Cabbage Palm
American Pasque	Ringnecked Pheasant	Black Hills Spruce
Iris	Mockingbird	Tulip Poplar
Bluebonet	Mockingbird	Pecan
Sego Lily	California Gull	Blue Spruce
Red Clover	Hermit Thrush	Sugar Maple
Flowering Dogwood	Cardinal	Flowering Dogwood
Coast Rhododendron	American Goldfinch	Western Hemlock
Rosebay Rhododendron	Cardinal	Sugar Maple
Butterfly Violet	Robin	Sugar Maple
Wyoming Paint Brush	Western Meadow Lark	Plains Cottonwood

ACKNOWLEDGEMENTS

I am indebted to the State executive offices and historical socie-
ties for invaluable information and material on the history of the
States. For their special efforts, I am particularly indebted to:

Governor William A. Egan of Alaska
Mr. James E. Jenkins, Director of Public Affairs, of California
Governor Thomas J. Meskill of Connecticut
Mr. Richard H. Caldwell, Asst. Secretary of State, of Delaware
Mr. Richard Stone, Secretary of State, of Florida
Mr. George R. Ariyoshi, Lt. Governor, of Hawaii
Governor Cecil D. Andrus of Idaho
Senator John Sherman Cooper of Kentucky
Senator Charles McC. Mathias, Jr. of Maryland
Mr. Jerry Bryan, Press Secretary, of Missouri
Governor Walter Peterson of New Hampshire
Mr. Francis R. O'Malley, Executive Dept., of New Jersey
Ms. Betty Fiorina, Secretary of State, of New Mexico
Mr. John P. Lomenzo, Secretary of State, of New York
Mr. Clyde Smith, Deputy Secretary of State, of North Carolina
Miss Lavene E. Good, of the State of Texas Office, Washington, D.C.
Mr. John A. Williams, Editor of State Papers, of Vermont
Mr. William P. Thaw, Deputy Secretary of State, of West Virginia
Governor Patrick J. Lucey of Wisconsin

For assistance and advice, I am indebted to:

Mr. Howard Berry and Mr. Donald Jodrie of Judd & Detweiler, Inc.
Dr. Robert F. Brockmann of the University of Maryland
Mr. Adron U. O'Neal of Beltsville, Maryland
Mrs. Brenda Smith of Glen Burnie, Maryland
Miss Liza J. Wilson of Wilson College
Miss Nan Yarnell of The Cricket Bookshop, Ashton, Maryland

Historian, writer and editor, Mr. Wilson is the author of *The Book of the Presidents* and *The Book of the Founding Fathers,* and editor of *The Book of Great American Documents,* which in 1968 was selected by the Freedoms Foundation at Valley Forge for its George Washington Honor Medal Award. In 1974 the Freedoms Foundation selected *The Book of the States* for its Honor Award. *The Book of the States* is also published in English/Japanese for use in schools in Japan. A native of Cleveland, Mr. Wilson studied at Cleveland's University School and at Georgetown, Arizona State, Claremont and Harvard.